# Yella Box

# & The ART of the EXIT

# DEMETRIUS MALONE

ISBN: 9781734634310

Demetrius Malone/ DemiCo National, LLC
3001 9th Avenue, SW
Huntsville, Alabama 35805

Editing: Lashonda M. Davidson
Cover Design: McKinley Harris
Photography: Steve Babin Photography

# TABLE OF CONTENTS

# INTRODUCTION

## CUSS WORDS

You're gonna have to learn how to cuss. Yep. Let's just start right there. I mean, I cussed everybody. It's true. Everybody! Demetrius Malone, the preacher's kid, the preacher himself, the timid and shy one - he lost it. He cussed everyone he passed on his way out of the prison, where he had spent his entire life. I surely did. I reached deep down into my suicidal and depressed soul, and let a beast lose. It was the only way.

While everyone else was trying to gather their minds around what had just occurred, I had made my exit. Let me be clear. As I left my toxic places, I cussed everyone on the road leading to and from the places that had inspired me to live a life of agony, defeat, and religious condemnation.

If I have already lost you and you are disturbed by the first tip, then I believe this book is not for you. That is fine. You may not be one of those to whom this book was specifically written. However, some of you who are reading this have been swallowing that cussing that has been trying to erupt from your lips for weeks, months, or even years. Some of you have already started cussing, but you got stuck there, and now you can't do anything but cuss. Let me explain.

I am not an advocate for cussing by any means, but sometimes cussing isn't even profanity. You would be surprised of the amount of people who have been conditioned to believe that the word "*NO*" is a cuss word. If you are going to take this journey with me, then you are going to have to be willing to take back your ability to cuss the things and people that have robbed you of your emotional, physical, and spiritual health.

By force, you have got to take back your *NO*, and you cannot be polite about it. Sometimes you cannot be a lady or a gentleman when taking back your *NO*. Sometimes you have to be a lion, and that roar from your mouth must let it be known that a violation has occurred that is not allowed. You need to be so good at saying "*NO*" that you can say "*Hell, No!*" when needed. If you want to stand any chance of exiting the toxic places in your life that consume you, then you are going to have to become comfortable saying some things you've never said before to some people who you have never said them to before. Trust me. Your life, freedom, and your pursuit of purpose is depending on your readiness to cuss anyone who dares to tread beyond the line you've drawn in the sand. You must note that people will not respect a line that has not been drawn.

I drew my exit in pencil during the spring of 2013 when I had the conversation with my ex-wife to inform her that our marriage was over. The union between two children of popular southern Baptist ministers, that seemingly would have been ideal, was ending. She had a blank look on her face, and she did not reply. I still do not think she thought I was serious at that moment. Everyone that knew me knew of the great love I once shared for this woman, and perhaps the idea that

I would be the one to end the relationship was unthought of. No one thought that I could or would leave her. While I think many people thought and still gambled on a possible divorce, everyone likely assumed she would leave me.

She had left me many times before while dating, and time and time again I welcomed her back with a new engagement ring. My love for her was never questioned by anyone who knew us. That meant something to me then. That still means something to me today. However, I knew that this was not the life that I believed God had for either of us, and I was no longer willing or able to try to further us down a road meant for a destined union.

If ever there was a marriage that God would save and sustain, surely it was my marriage - so I thought. Before this moment, divorce had never crossed my mind. I had never seen divorce among my parents, siblings, grandparents, aunts, or uncles. While this isn't to suggest that everyone in my family had perfect or harmonious marriages, but for whatever reason, everyone for generations of my maternal and paternal families had shied away from divorce. So, for me to be the lone wolf about to tread a path unknown to those closest to me, I initially felt as if I was weaker than the rest of my family.

We were nearing seven years in a sexless and loveless marriage, and by this time, I had already begun healing. You see, I did not divorce Tonya to heal. I divorced her because I healed, and I took my healing seriously. She needed to find healing as well, whether she knew it or not. So, I gave her my plan to remain in the house for the next six months while we prepared financially, emotionally, and spiritually for the exit.

Over the six months, I obtained greater peace with each passing day. Somewhere around month three, I began trying to have discussions of splitting belongings, property, and ordinary things that couples normally would fight over during a split. She remained silent. However, I was no longer angry. So, I assumed that if we could establish some sense of peace and understanding before the big exit, that once the world found out of our separation, we would be in control emotionally.

I had spent years miserable. Tonya had spent years miserable, and now it was all nearing an end. As we neared the exit date, I entered the kitchen to apologize. I felt my tears building, and my voice trembling before I made it through the first sentence. I needed to apologize and ask for her forgiveness. I put her in a position that I knew she did not belong. My marriage perhaps could be described as one to the most toxic relationships imaginable, but you have to understand something.

You have to get this one thing before we go any further. The toxic relationship that is killing you is not with another individual. It is not your toxic spouse, your parents, friend, sibling, boss, pastor, or neighbor. The toxicity in them provides them with the credentials to be to the jail-keepers to the prisons in your life that you do not share with others. Until that is understood, you will spend the next 60 years of your life in the same cell, but with different wardens.

"It was my fault. I proposed to you three times before you finally said yes. I knew you weren't ready. I knew I wasn't ready. I knew it wasn't right," I said as she continued washing dishes. Again, she said nothing. "I'm trying to do this in the best possible way to avoid drama, and it getting ugly. It doesn't have to get ugly. We can do this the right way."

"It's gonna get ugly!", She promised while rinsing a knife from the soap water and stabbing it into the knife block. One might think that would have been the inclination for me to remove the knives from the house; however, it was not. In that moment, my mind was elsewhere.

She was the woman I married, but she was the third woman to whom I had proposed marriage. The next night we took the kids out to dinner. It was a relatively new Mexican restaurant we all enjoyed. I was nervous, and she was still silent. That night, with all our hands reaching for the same bowl of salsa, I drew with permanent pen on my exit.

I told the children I was moving out. It was now real. There would be no backing out. I would not cast the confusion of the separation on the children to only return and change my mind days later, completely robbing them of security and structure. I had experienced that myself as a child, so if I told them I was leaving, then I would leave. So, the next day, I did. For the first time in my life, I walked away from something that did not, would not, and could not honor me. It felt magical. It felt like a giant splash of yellow. But I did have to cuss on my way out. I had to cuss everyone aiming to block my exit with religious dogmas, social statistics, and manipulation. While it did alarm me, it felt good. It tasted better than steak, and it felt better than sex. Whether I used four-letter words or not, I said the words I was not supposed to say.

One of the most painful moments in life is when you realize that many of the people you thought were your cellmates were never your cellmates, sharing in the same pursuit of spiritual, emotional, and mental freedom. Instead, many of them were the jail-keepers. How could I be so broken that every single person in my life was a jail-keeper working endlessly to keep me in my prison?

I had built an entire life full of jail-keepers. Now I was a fugitive from the place that destroyed me while friends, family, and even fellow clergy, all patrolled to return me to my prison. Once it was realized that I would not return, then I lost everything. You see, all jail-keepers know that they are jail-keepers; they do not want to be labeled jail-keepers. They much more prefer the label: *loved ones who protect*. I was not just leaving my wife. I was leaving the toxic prisons that influenced and allowed me to marry a woman I knew did not love me. I had been in this place since I was five years old, and the sudden exit was causing the walls to crumble down around me as I raced away.

Feeling myself breaking from the very brink of my sanity, I could no longer endure the rumors, attacks, and tears. I needed relief. I needed to say something I had never said before to some people I had never said it to before. With my phone ringing and text messages dinging from the news of the separation, I needed to cuss. I needed that sweet relief, but there was no one to cuss now. I was not falling apart because of the end of my marriage, but because I was at the end of the prison, and only I knew what sentenced me to the prison. The moment for me to address why I was sentenced to that prison had come, and for the first time in my entire life, it had to be acknowledged. I had to cuss my fucking self and say it.

Flooded with memories of a childhood with panic attacks, depression and more, I knew that I was nearing a breakdown. Driving, I raced to get the last of my boxes to my new apartment before imploding. I was less than ten miles from the exit closest to what would be my new home when I realized that I would not make it to the apartment in time. With my face tingling, and sweat pouring down my back, I eventually did not take the closest exit, but the safest exit.

I hurried my car from the ramp and into the parking lot of a McDonalds. Looking around, I recognized the SUV turning into the parking lot. The car belonged to Pastor Martin. She was a dear colleague and friend in which I loved as a mother. I was sure that by now she had heard of the separation and if she saw me, she would surely want to pray, pray, and pray. Even though she was in objection to my marriage to my wife, she had fallen for the performance of a happy marriage. Pastor Martin would unquestionably believe that I was letting Satan destroy a beautiful marriage. I was not in the mood to pray. I needed to cuss, dammit. So, as my hyperventilating increased, I compromised and prayed that she wouldn't see me, approach me, and I cuss her. Within moments her car vanished in a sea of sedans. I parked, turned the rearview mirror to my face, exhaled, and I cussed. I cussed me.

"I was molested." There was a silence that seemed to last just as long as the shame. I looked at myself.

"What did you say?" A voice said from the car. Unable to remember when I had dialed or began conversing, I recognized my mother's voice sounding through my car's speaker system. I gasped for air. "He said he was molested". I heard her repeat to my father. There was a knock on the passenger's door window. It was Pastor Martin. I shut off the engine, gripped the steering wheel, ignored Pastor Martin, and I cussed again.

"Mama, from age five to nine, I was molested." And just like that, bam! The exit began.

# CHAPTER ONE

## HOW TO KNOW IF YOU ARE IN A TOXIC RELATIONSHIP

I'm pretty sure that by now you have realized that I am preparing to share with you my story and my strategy for saving my life by leaving the toxic relationships that I craved with such desire, that I would have chosen death over deliverance. A few times, I did choose death over deliverance, death just refused to choose me. As I ready for this journey, I ask you to do one thing. Do not allow me to embark on this journey without you. I ask that you do not further through this tale of misadventures to only conclude in the end that I was speaking to everyone else but you. If you have continued reading unto this page, then it is my belief that you are exactly where you need to be for a life-altering experience for you and those you love.

Where do we begin? That is simple. How to know if you are in a toxic relationship? Over the past ten years, with a mass amount of YouTubers now pursuing public speaker career paths, we often hear people oh so casually speak of toxic relationships. First, this must be said. Instead of learning conflict resolution skills, many people will wrongfully label anything they do not like as toxic to justify their desire to be selfish or pursue what they perceive as self-care. Real toxic relationships do exist. We hear tales of the toxic spouse or friend. Those individuals certainly carry the stereotype of toxic relationships. However, what happens when the toxicity choking your chance at happiness is coming from your parent, pastor, boss, or even your own child? What happens when the poison comes from the people who are socially mandated to occupy time and space in your life?

I believe that seeds of shame are planted into our souls from birth to our late teens. The next sixty years of our lives are filled with people aiming to water, nourish and cultivate those seeds, or people aiming to remove the seeds. Every person you meet in this life can be placed into one of those two groups. It is your responsibility to become so self-aware that you can identify in a matter of minutes those who come to water your seeds of shame, versus those who have come to remove those seeds.

Most of the time we pledge our hearts and loyalty to those who knowingly or unknowingly water the seeds of shame in our lives. It's never our intent, but usually, the seeds of shame have been planted so deeply within our internal essence that it is easier to embrace someone who hurts us versus someone who heals us. You can lie to me, cheat me, abuse me, and misuse me. Just don't force me to heal me. Many of us carry this idea with us throughout our entire lives. So, I want to begin with the question that I am asked daily: How do I know if I am in a toxic relationship?

First, you must understand the difference between a bad period, a bad relationship, and a toxic relationship. These are three very different relationships. If you were to buy your brand-new luxury dream car, you must always remember that even the best of cars drive poorly when they happen upon a bumpy road. You would be surprised of the amount of people who have traded in good cars simply because they drove poorly in a bad situation. It is up to you to know the difference between a bad car and a bad road. As long as the car is in good shape, the road will eventually smooth or you can exit onto another road. However, if the car is bad it will be bad regardless of the road on which it is driven until it is repaired. But a toxic car is much worse than a bad car. It poses threats to your overall safety, security, and most of all, your destination. Let's go further.

### Poor Communication

While all issues of poor communication are not always an indication of a toxic relationship; it is the first sign that emotional chaos is on the horizon. This will certainly not be a book that cast all emotional hang-ups on the shoulders of our parents, but the liberty or lack thereof to communicate our feelings as children follows us all into adulthood. Remember, everyone you meet as adults will either nourish the seeds of shame or remove the seeds. All of our romantic relationships are directly linked to our paternal relationships. So, if your parents absolutely banned self-expression and your ability to communicate your feelings to them as a child without consequence, you must begin questioning if God would send someone else into your adulthood to further nourish that same seed of shame?

The inability to effectively communicate is perhaps the first sign of toxicity among your relationships. It is of the utmost importance that we understand we communicate not only with our words, but also with our body language. Typically, the individual suffering the most from the toxic relationship tends to be the one attempting to communicate the most, but to no avail. The jail-keepers usually do not complain often. They are typically inwardly at ease until the individual in agony speaks on their pain. Communication is the greatest form of respect to any relationship; be it romantic, platonic, or even professional. When communication ceases to exist, inevitably the foundation of the relationship crumbles, and the relationship itself will begin to crumble. When you no longer have communication, all that you will have left is your imagination; and my friend, an imagination is a deadly thing to have when there is no outlet for communication.

I learned at a young age to keep a secret and avoid communication. The first year of my molestation had passed, and it was now a routine for my young life and my young body. The late 80's were much different times for families. Kids played outside, rode bikes, ventured into the woods, and enjoyed sleepovers. When readying for bed at a family slumber party during the late 80s, I innocently spoke out as all the kids made their way to their pillows and blankets. I was perhaps the youngest and very sleepy.

"We gonna all have sex before we go to bed?", I casually asked, being the youngest of the children. Immediately, the other children laughed and were shocked.

"What the fuck did he just say?"

"Yella Box, you crazy."

"What's wrong with him?" They laughed.

While they thought I had lost my young mind and eventually returned to a pillow fight; I glanced at the nervousness on my teenaged molester's face who was now fearing being exposed. It was at that moment when my six-year-old mind realized I was not supposed to be having sex. This was not supposed to be happening to me. It had never crossed my mind that what was happening to me was vile, disgusting, and sick. But, because they laughed, I locked it away, and it would stay there for the next 24 years. But who influenced me to keep it a secret? Did my molester threaten me? Did he tell me to keep it a secret? No. Liquid foundation taught me to keep a secret. Every Sunday morning as she allowed me to sit on her bed to change her purse items from her casual purse to her church purse, my mother would ask me to give her the liquid foundation. I was always amazed that my mother's beautiful skin could be copied into a small finger size jar. Standing in her bathroom mirror with the staticky gospel radio station blaring, she would dab a bit in her palm and then spread it across her face. Within a matter of moments, the signs of my father's fist were gone from her face. Upon leaving the bathroom, she would ask me,

"How do I look, Meme?" Even at the age of six, I would feel my future manhood decaying every time I gave her what she asked me for; but she was my queen. So, I gave her all I had to give. I gave her what I thought she needed. I gave her my approval.

"You look good." And just like that, the nights before were erased and never discussed. So, liquid foundation taught me how to keep abuse hidden.

Many times in a toxic relationship, the individual who is being emotionally or physically abused begins placing unrealistic expectations on themselves. Whether dealing with an abusive friend, family member or spouse, do you ever find yourself saying, "I'm just not going to say anything else about it?" This is the first sign that you have lost hope in the ability to communicate with someone. You have likely by this time had multiple conversations about the things that are hurting you, and after failing to see progress, you did what we as humans naturally do: we flip a safety switch. Some call it defense mechanisms. However, you refer to it, we all make internal adjustments to situations that give us pause.

'Fine. I just won't say anything else; we tell ourselves. So now, every time that you are hurt, you find yourself swallowing this mountain of pain, trying to keep a vow of silence that you never should have made to yourself. You are not turning off the pain switch, you are turning off the red light that shows others pain has occurred.

What has likely happened by this point, is that you have unsuccessfully tried to communicate an issue to your partner which results in an all-out war. You are left feeling as if you are making a big deal out of nothing. You are left feeling as if there is something mentally and emotionally wrong with you because of your feelings.

Then you find yourself dropping the issue and possibly spending the rest of the night asking yourself, "Why do I do that?" Why do I keep talking about that? "Why do I bring this hurt on myself when I know he/she will not do anything differently?" You are punishing yourself for screaming when you are being stabbed. A toxic person will act as if you are the first one to complain about a behavior they have that others have complained about to them for years.

This is an unbelievably dangerous game to play with yourself which begins to cause you to blame yourself for the failed communication. If you are in a toxic relationship with someone, there is no right or wrong way to tell them something they do not wish to hear, you must realize their issue may not be what you are saying, but rather the fact that it is you who is saying it. People who cannot communicate, think that everything is an argument. Do you find yourself spending extra time planning how to present, discuss, or communicate an issue with someone to avoid an angry, aggressive, and hostile conflict? Do you find yourself sitting at work, driving your car, or cooking dinner planning how to discuss something that is troubling you in a way that does not cause a war?

I believe that the first thing in a person will always be the first thing out of a person. Imagine a glass of ice water with a floating lemon in the glass. If the lemon is at the top of the glass, then chances are your straw will strike the sour lemon first. But, if the lemon is midways down the glass beneath several cubes of ice, then you have to hit water and ice before hitting that sour lemon. My point is that we all have sourness in us, but it shouldn't be the first thing out of you. People should have to poke through the water then through the ice before they hit the sour part of you. If tolerance, understanding, patience, and love is the first thing in you, then it will be the first thing out of you.

When talking with the individual who may be toxic with jail-keeper tendencies, do you find yourself feeling poorly about hurting them by discussing the things done that hurt you? Pay close attention to the next conversation in which you address your pains. You should not have to fill your complaint with tons of positive affirmations of them to sweeten the sour words into being more tolerable by them.

While communicating, it is important that you notice the shift of power game. When someone knows he or she made a mistake, but has no intentions to own their failure, they immediately begin waiting for you to make a mistake in your delivery and then play victim. Now you find yourself no longer discussing the act that hurt you but apologizing for how you may have communicated that you were hurt. Manipulative people like to play victim to the situations they created. If you find yourself feeling that the relationship would be perfect if you stopped discussing what hurts you, then you have already lost a valuable part of your heart, mind, and soul to the relationship. It is time for a change.

I was raised by strict southern parents who were born during the early fifties. Like many of you, our childhood homes were never conducive for communicating our emotions. I always believed my father interpreted any opinions or feelings other than his own as disrespect. He was born during a time that children had no voice. I was absolutely terrified of my father my entire childhood. To tell the truth, I still had terrifying dreams of him on into my early or mid-twenties. Let me stop and clarify that my father was not my molester. Frankly, my father's wrath would have split the world in half had I told him at such a young age that I was being raped. As a child, my dad was massive. He was huge, and I tensed whenever he entered the kitchen door.

From the moment I would hear his large key chain hit and slide across the kitchen countertop, until the next morning when I left for school, I was scared stiff. To me, his voice was bigger than God's. When he would yell, which was constantly, it seemed as if the entire house would shake.

He and my mother argued a lot. The arguments were abusive and being the youngest; I would have to see that my mom was okay. At times, while three of my siblings seemed to not hear or be troubled by the battles, one of my brothers would resort to turning on programming from the TBN Network as loud as the television would sound. Doing so, I could not make out the words of the argument. I could not determine if my mother was okay. I would camp out at the bedroom door.

Knowing there was nothing I could do; I still had to hear even though I hated hearing. I remember the moment in which I did hear my father say he was moving out. I could hear the sound of the wire hangers sliding across the metal closet rack as he pulled his Sunday suits and belongings from the closet. As much as I feared him, I knew he loved us. There was never any question of his love for us. My mom was an enormous fan of *Days of Our Lives*. I had made a habit of pretending to be sick mornings after they had massive fights so I could stay home with her. I don't know if she thought I was truly sick, or if she knew I was faking, and just needed me close. We would watch the fictional town of Salem as its residents tried to survive the evil deeds of supervillain, Stefano Dimera. He was a ruthless, brutal, and large tyrant who loved his family to no end. But he was deadly, and his family feared him.

I would see my dad when I would see Stefano. I would see Stefano when I would see my dad. In fact, I would see my dad in every daytime soap. We would also watch *The Young & The Restless, Another World*, and other daytime soaps. One thing I noticed was every show chronicled a wealthy, powerful, and abusive man who terrified all those around him, but loved his children. My dad's presence was monumental at home, the business he owned, and even the church he pastored. He was not respected. He was feared.

The night he said he was leaving would become the first night I would suffer a panic attack. Although I had not told him that I was being molested, it gave me some sort of peace just to hope that all I had to do was say the word, and he would save me. But I couldn't say the word, and because of his own demons, he couldn't see that there were words that I needed to speak. I raced to the bedroom, where the younger children slept to inform my brothers that he was packing and moving out. I began to cry. They did not take the threat seriously, or maybe they were just sleepy because the arguments never occurred until after midnight on school nights. We had become accustomed to waking up to loud shouting matches.

After a few more hours the argument silenced, and he stayed. So, naturally we all struggled to get dressed for school this next morning. I became irritated at my mother for not knowing why we were so sluggish about readying for school. However, my entire school day was consumed with the image of his clothes still scattered across the living room sofa as we left the house for school. I assumed that meant that moving out was still on the table for him. By the time I made it home from school, the clothes had returned to the closet, and we all had half an hour to eat dinner and jump into the family van for the 45-minute drive to the church for Bible Study where Dad pastored.

My Mom, a teacher, had implemented tutoring services and homework assistance at the church. So, while the adults would enjoy Bible Study, the kids would complete their homework and act a fool. That day she cooked lemon pepper pork chops. It was Dad's favorite meal, and it always followed major fights. After eating, I went to my bedroom to gather my backpack. When passing my parents' bedroom, I noticed Dad's clothes had not been returned to the closet, but rather the bed. I wasn't sure why the clothes had not made it two feet from the bed to the closet, so I interpreted that as meaning he would leave following our return from church that night. Also, in that moment it registered in my young mind that the fights amongst my parents only occurred during the times in which I was not being raped. I wondered if the two were somehow connected. I had heard my Dad preach sermons on the games and tricks Satan uses to trap you. Could this be my trap? I wondered if I were to choose being raped over my mother's abuse, would she be saved? My young mind attempted to reason if such a transaction could be made, and since Marlena had just told John that he had made a deal with the devil, Stefano, then perhaps, I too could make a deal.

I grabbed my backpack from my bed and headed into the backyard to where my molester worked on one of my Dad's cars. Let's just refer to him as Jeff.

"I want to have sex sometime," I said as he stood on a crate leaning under the hood over the engine."

"Get yo' faggot yella ass away from me before I kick your ass," Jeff said jumping from the crate onto the gravel. He kicked gravel at me. I don't know why kicking gravel at me absolutely broke my heart, but it did. Maybe it was because I had seen my brothers chase away stray dogs from my grandmother's land the same way. I turned and hurried back into the house.

Unable to imagine a house or a life without my Dad, in that moment I was tired. I mean, this was a tiredness that a child of such a young age should never know. I was tired from the sole of my little feet to the crown of my yellow head. I was tired, and I wanted relief; I was ready to die. So, as my brother Cedric raced one of my dad's many cars into the driveway to avoid being late for church, I made my way behind the car. I inhaled, shed a tear, told God I loved him, and closed my eyes to prepare for the impact.

My mother canceled Bible Study as my Dad lifted me from the bloody driveway.

### *The Blame Game*

What are more indications that you are in a toxic relationship? Well, the blame game is undoubtedly an indication of such. When it comes to behaviors that screw up your relationships, blaming the other person for something – justified or not; it is a clear sign of a toxic and unhealthy relationship. Personally, this is one that I kept seeing recycle itself in many relationships in my life.

Chronic blaming is a highly dangerous form of emotional abuse. Chronically being blamed for an act that you did not actually commit is like taking a verbal beating. It leaves you not only shocked to be accused but bewildered that your loved one could place such blame on your shoulders. Even if this was something that you actually were responsible for but meant no harm, constantly getting blamed is still an inappropriate and non-productive form of communication between lovers, friends, or family members.

I believe that there are two sides to every story, but you should always question the side of the story that has been in this story many times before. Some people can continue having the same dysfunctional interaction with person after person for years, but always blame others. Our self-esteem is not built to sustain repeated blames, whether they are accurate or not.

Most of the time, we as people do not share what we feel; we share what we think. For example, a jealous spouse may share that they think you are unfaithful. However, what they feel is a sense of inadequacy, fear of not being enough, and anxiety of being alone. Instead, they will likely accuse or blame you of the things that are easiest for them to address.

Blaming murders intimacy. It's obviously difficult to get close to someone or to maintain a close relationship when they have their arm outstretched with an accusing finger.

### Subtle Jealousy

Granted, at first, the jealousy was probably flattering. You probably thought it was cute. You probably even bragged about it to your friends. You likely read it as a declaration of their desire to let the world know you were together. You probably believed it was an assuring act of letting you know that they only have eyes only for you. After time progressed, you may have begun to notice the jealousy was no longer charming, but now your prison.

While most of us commonly think jealousy is just an emotion experienced between romantic partners, I can surely object. Toxicity has no respect of persons, so you have to be careful not to be imprisoned by jealousy from your parents, siblings, boss, or even your pastor. Yes, even pastors have been known to exemplify some of the worst toxic tendencies known imaginable.

### Your Decisions vs Our Decisions

They constantly want to play a part in any decision you make. They just can't seem to accept it if you choose to do something that does not have their approval.

### My Possessiveness is Love

Every time you point out just how possessive they are, they defend themselves by claiming they are possessive only because they love and care about you so much.

### Stalking

They stalk you or try to find out where you are often when you're out with a friend by calling you up out of the blue and telling you they want to see you or meet you, or that they want to pick you up.

### No New Experiences

They are extremely protective about you and don't want you to do anything new without them. They behave like your life is in danger when they are not around to take care of you, and sulks when you try something new for the first time without them.

### They See Red

They get really mad over simple issues, especially if it involves someone they fear may expose them or liberate you. They just don't want you to create any memories or do anything fun with anyone but them.

### Inquisitive

They are extremely inquisitive about everything that goes on in your life. And if you don't talk about something you consider too trivial to talk about, they get angry or sulk until you tell them all the details, all the time.

### Time

It doesn't matter who you're talking to, but they expect you to answer their call as soon as they call you even if you're busy on another call. And if you ignore them because you're busy, they accuse you of ignoring them or being a poor mate. They expect you to carve out time for them regardless of what is going on in your life.

They have sentenced you to spend all of your time with them. Often, toxic people use the time they spend with you to gauge your mental space and determine how closely they have you wrapped around their little finger. The longer you avoid interaction, the more upset he/she will become because they cannot measure their control over you. They will do seemingly nice things for you during times in which they know you are busy, preoccupied, or with others such as cooking dinner or buying gifts, that now require you to have to spend time with them. If you do not, they make you feel guilty for all of their hard work put towards doing something special for you that you were too busy to acknowledge.

### *Controlling*

They do not like it if you meet a friend or go out anywhere without telling them about it first, even if they are not around. It starts small until you find yourself asking them for permission for everything you do.

### *Everyone Else in Your Life Is Flawed*

They ridicule all your friends, colleagues, and family, and constantly picks at their flaws. Every time your friend or family let you down, they take it upon themselves to emphasize just how unreliable they are, and how he/she's the one you can completely trust. They will always remind you that they knew the person who disappointed you would disappoint you. This is to build themselves up as a source of consultation for you when choosing friends.

Pay close attention to this one, especially if you are a spiritual individual. Often, a manipulator will fill your ears with their claims of revelations from God warning you against people they personally want out of your life. A narcissist can enter a room and have 999 people eating out of the palm of their hands, but he or she will obsess over the 1 who is not. The narcissist will fear the 1 sees he or she as they truly are and will expose them to the 999. So, the narcissist will attack the 1 and cry victim to the 999 and encourage the 999 to believe the 1 is against them all. This is the narcissist's game to secure his or her position of control over the 999.

### They Hate Space

The idea of giving each other space shocks them. They want to be a part of everything you do, and yet, they may whine and nag about something you enjoy until you give it all up altogether.

### Their World Revolves Around You

They behave like their entire life revolves around you, and they force you to behave the same way around them, even if you don't feel that way just yet. They want to be the center of your world and force you to give them preferential attention over everyone else in your life. Anyone whose life revolves around you, will expect the same from you in return.

### The Tag Along

He/she is extremely insecure however hard you try to make them feel loved. They do not like it when you go out to meet your friends by yourself, and always insist on tagging along, but makes it obvious to you that they are uncomfortable and ready to leave.

## *Compliments*

They do not like it when you speak highly of someone else. Every time you say something nice about a friend or a family member, they immediately try to point out the individual's flaws. He/she is extremely competitive and wants you to believe that they are the only one you should ever look up to or seek help.


Twenty-eight years later, and my parents still have not referred to the driveway incident as my suicide attempt. I waited for them to do so for many years, but they did not. Perhaps, it was because they could not. Sometimes during his sermons, my dad would regularly speak of my silly decision to stand behind a moving car almost with laughter. Truthfully, I don't think he could see the reality. So, after a few days of recovering, and the swelling leaving my legs, I returned to school.

My teacher welcomed me back with a massive embrace. It felt great, but her perfume was always extremely strong, and when she pulled me in for a hug, she would bury my face between her breasts. Mrs. Gladden was a friend of my mother, so I assumed my mother had called her and gave her some version of the incident. I just wanted to get back to school and get to work on the play that I was writing. Feeling drained and my legs throbbing in pain, I knew I would not be able to participate in P.E.

I knew that if I told Mrs. Gladden I was not feeling well, she would disregard my complaint because surely my mom would not have sent me back to school in less than perfect condition. To avoid P.E., I might have to tell her my version of the story, and I was now okay with that. As a matter of fact, I might just tell her everything, I thought. Yes, that's it. The raping, suicide attempt, and her perfume smelling like a damn Sharpie; I will tell her everything. I knew I would cry, and I did not want to cry. So, I would write it in a letter, and that is what I did. I wrote it in a letter, folded it with my spelling test, and placed it upside down on my desk as we were always instructed to do when finished with our tests. I exhaled.

I watched her like a hawk as I waited for her to pick up the test. My best friend, Charles, sat next to me. While I was always racing to turn in my work first, he always seemed to be in a race to be the last kid even to get started. Mrs. Gladden became increasingly annoyed with him. I was growing annoyed as well because his inability to spell was causing her to wait to discover my plea for help.

Mrs. Oliff, the teacher's aide, began watching me. I felt as if she could see through me. I became fearful that she would intercept my letter. She was so nice and kind, but weak. Mrs. Gladden bullied her, and all the kids knew it. She would speak to her so harshly in our presence. Sometimes, Mrs. Oliff would cry. Mrs. Gladden stood over Charles' desk.

"Boy, what is taking you so long? I ain't gone repeat this word no' mo." She said. She exhaled and then repeated it again. "House, boy. How do you spell house?"

"Can you use it in a sentence?" Charles asked without looking at her.

"Did you hear that?" Mrs. Gladden laughed to Mrs. Oliff. "He asked me to use house in a sentence," She said. Mrs. Oliff gave a fake laugh. Mrs. Gladden kneeled over to Charles, putting her behind practically on my desk and murmured, "House. Charles, why don't you come over to my house and we'll have sex?"

My heart skipped a beat. She laughed and stood straight. Mrs. Oliff looked at me, and once Mrs. Gladden saw the look on her face, she knew that I overheard her remark. She stopped laughing.

I looked at Charles. He continued writing and did not look up. He did not look at Mrs. Gladden, and he did not look at me. He continued as if nothing had occurred. Mrs. Gladden neared me and her perfume burned my nostrils.

"Meme, why are you looking at me like that?", she asked with her hand on her hip. She had never referred to me by my family nickname. I spoke.

"I heard what you said to him."

"What did I say?" She said, stepping closer. I looked at Mrs. Oliff. Her eyes were pleading with me to not answer. No one had ever protected me, and I could not do that to someone else.

"You told him to come over to your house and have sex," I stated before she slapped me across my back. Mrs. Oliff screamed. The room was quiet as the other kids looked at me. My eyes filled with tears. Charles still avoided looking up.

"Get your test and bring it. You're working in the hall for the rest of the day. You don't cuss in my classroom!! You wait until I tell Rev. Malone you in here lying." Gasping for air, I stood, grabbed my test, my loneliness, and my confession and carried it all into the hall.

# CHAPTER TWO

## INDENTIFYING THE DAMAGE DONE

Now that you may have come to the realization that you are in a toxic relationship, it is now time to identify exactly what the relationship has cost you emotionally, spiritually, professionally, socially, and even financially. What price has your self-esteem paid so that you could maintain this relationship? How has your views of God, or a power greater than yourself, been shifted or altered as a result of the constant toxicity in your life? Where did all of your friends or family go? The truth is that every relationship has a cost. Sometimes the cost is patience, forgiveness, and understanding, and that is fine. However, if the relationship prohibits you from being the truest most healed version of yourself, then you must realize the cost is you. You are selling yourself to buy the relationship, and you cannot afford that.

Whether in business or relationships, you must never invest more than you can afford to lose. If no one has told you before, then I will tell you now: you cannot afford to lose you. The world cannot afford to lose you. Anything there is only one of in existence, is priceless. It is likely that if you have spent a great deal of time in this relationship then you have already begun to notice the damage it has caused in your life.

All relationships have the potential to become toxic in the wrong setting. Imagine a single mother, let's call her Pam. Pam cooks a great pot of spaghetti. After her young kids eat, she places the leftover spaghetti in Tupperware and sits it in the fridge. Days go by, and weeks pass. Pam knows that the spaghetti has now gone bad and is toxic, but instead of removing it from the fridge, she leaves it. Months go by, and Pam would not dare eat from the source she knows is now toxic. The problem is that she knows it is toxic, but she never communicated that it was toxic to those in the house who trust what she puts in the refrigerator. While Pam would never eat what is now poison, little Tommy does eat it because even a child assumes that if it wasn't any good, his mother would have thrown it out.

This is what happens when we raise children in toxic places after we have flipped on a numbing switch. Your child interprets the presence you allow around them to be a presence worthy of being around them. The child assumes you are emotionally healthy enough to avoid bringing poison into their space. While you may know certain behaviors of your spouse, friend or parent are not to be ingested, your child will absorb everything you place in the safe space for them. Whatever you put up with is what you will end up with.

Upon my divorce in 2013, I realized that practically every relationship I had since birth had been toxic. My parents, a teacher, a pedophile relative, and even my tainted views of God were all toxic. So, it was inevitable that I would marry a woman who could only keep me comfortable in the prisons I had been in since my childhood. And since she was the one to whom I pledged my heart and soul, she had to be the accumulation of all toxic people and places I had met along the way. However, she was not the first. I married her, but I had proposed to many other women before finally marrying Tonya.

So, what was the damage done from a toxic relationship with my parents? I am still learning the damage today. You see, I believe that whenever a new opportunity to progress and be happy presents itself in life, all the ways in which we need to heal always rise to the surface to show their heads. So, the more I prosper, grow and obtain success, the more I will discover areas that I am not healed. But I did notice enough damage in me to know that it was time to exit all the people, places, things, and ideas that carried over from my childhood.

As a kid, had I known that weekly or monthly threats to move out by my mother and father would become a childhood norm, maybe I wouldn't have tried to kill myself to keep my Dad from leaving. By the time I was ten, I had my own plastic grocery store bag packed beneath my bed waiting for my mom to level up and move out. I was ready to exit; she was not.

Perhaps, I did worship her. She was perfect to me. She was beautiful, and she saw so much potential in me that I felt my father never saw. Both of my parents were entrepreneurs during most of my life. While I despised many things about my father, his work ethic, ambition, and creativity raised all his five sons to all be dreamers, entrepreneurs, and visionaries. However, I never quite grasped some of the mechanics he worked so hard to instill within us. Not because I was incapable, but because I hated being around grown men by this time. It had become a regular and common thing for grown men to, in secret, make sexual remarks towards me, and it scared the living shit out of me. So, I always nestled myself under my mother because I felt safe there. My anxiety by this time was crippling me and it was becoming noticeable.

Another Sunday morning, while standing in my mother's bathroom with her as she painted the previous night's bruises away again, I did not even notice that she and my Dad were arguing. Perhaps, the blaring gospel radio station distracted me, or maybe I was becoming used to the fights by now. The arguing continued until my father pulled a rotating fan from the dresser, snatching the cord from the wall, and hurling it at the bathroom. My mother pushed me to the side, screamed, and slammed the door closed as the fan crashed into the door. I struggled to focus my eyes. I had hit my head on the ceramic toilet tissue holder.

"You're crazy! You could have cut my head off with that damn fan!", she shouted to him as she opened the bathroom door. I froze. The idea that my father could have done something that would have cut my mother's head off terrified me. What if she had not pushed me out of the way in time or slammed the door closed to protect us? It was as if they could not see me. I walked pass her and ran from their bedroom. I felt dizzy. The arguing continued on into the living room where I saw him lift her from her feet as he choked her. I could not speak, move, or scream out. I froze, as did my brother Dowand standing next to me. He eventually let her go, and he walked fast back to their bedroom. He passed us in the hall, as if he could not see us.

She chased behind him also as if she could not see us, until she passed out on the floor at our feet. My brother cried and knelt to her as I just stared. I was certain she was dead. I was certain he had killed her.

Janice Strong was a cousin on my Dad's side (we did not see my mother's family often). Janice had two young daughters and a son. While I had not seen the kids since we left the family church and Dad began pastoring his own church, I always thought my cousins were nice and could sing. Weeks prior to watching my mother collapse at my feet, the slain bodies of Janice and her children were all found in their home by a neighbor. Janice's abusive boyfriend had resulted to using a tire iron to kill her and her young children. Of Janice's three children, one survived. Most of the family attended the funeral, which consisted of three coffins spread across the altar. I was too terrified to attend the funeral. The night following the discovery of the bodies, while frying chicken, my mother spoke that she would not be surprised if we would all be next. I am not sure if she was speaking to me, herself, my Dad, or anyone else in the house, but I heard the words as I sat in the living room chair closest to the kitchen as I wrote a new story.

So, when she collapsed at my feet, I thought she was right. He had killed her, and he would come after us next. Instead, she eventually stood. She made her way into their bedroom and slammed the door in our faces. We continued onto church that morning, still as if nothing happened. We sang, preached, worshipped and portrayed as we always did. By this time people were traveling from miles away to hear the Malone Brothers sing. Dowand and Dewayne were around eleven years old, and Dowand was the celebrity kid preacher thrusting the family further into the spotlight. We were considered the gospel *Jackson Five*.

Weeks would pass, and I couldn't pretend any further. As my father prayed, sweated, and proclaimed God's protection of his wife and children my anxiety consumed me, my head ached, and I fainted. There he stood illustrating the evils in the world that would lead to the heinous murders of Janice and her children, and my mind could not keep up with my ears. So, my body became exhausted. Again, my eight-year-old body was unconscious and awakening to what I was sure was death. I struggled to focus my eyes as I was being rushed from the heat of the sanctuary. I could hear the voices of my mother and father panicking. The sunlight hit my face as I was carried into the parking lot. There was air, but it wasn't fresh air. It was filled with nothing that made me feel as if I was alive.

"Get him some air."

"Meme, open your eyes! Open your eyes."

"Yella Box, you okay?"

"Do we need to call an ambulance?"

The voices echoed around me. My mother's cries were piercing me, and I wanted to keep my heavy eyelids open to assure her that I was alive. So, with all my might, I forced my eyes open to see Jeff carrying me. As much as I hated for him to touch me, there he was touching me in the middle of the church, and no one saved me. Granted, no one knew the truth, but a part of my young self died at that moment because the God I was taught could move mountains, part seas, and raise the dead, could not open the eyes to all these people to what was right in front of their eyes. I realized shortly after that no one would come to save me. I didn't even know what saving me looked like, but I knew it would not happen. I knew that the responsibility to protect myself would be solely on my own shoulders. I struggled to find a plan to protect myself, but violence was all that I knew. Jeff was everywhere. He was at our church, our home, and even my Dad's mechanic garage.

A few days after I fainted, my mother decided to grill porkchops for my Dad. I watched her drown the charcoal in lighter fluid. She did not have matches, so she crumbled a brown paper bag and held it to the stove top until it lit in flames. She then raced from the kitchen, through the living room, out the back door and dropped the torch in the grill. As I stood in the kitchen, I saw Jeff step from a truck with my father. He made his way into the house and towards the bathroom. I looked at the lighter fluid on the countertop, another empty brown paper bag, and the red stovetop burner. I became angry that I was in the house alone with him. I could almost smell his rotten breath by looking at him. Perhaps, he did not even know I was in the house, but dammit I was angry. I crumbled the bag, held it to the burner and grabbed the lighter fluid. I began to cry as I raced from the kitchen with the burning paper bag. I felt the flames nearing my hand as I raced towards the bathroom. Realizing I would not make it to Jeff, I dropped the burning bag and the shag carpet lit on fire. Jeff raced into the living room at the same time as my mother while I fought to extinguish the fire. The flames died, but the house was filled with smoke. I stood over the black burnt hole in the carpet. I saw my father nearing the back door and I knew what was next. I could not speak of what I was doing. My Dad removed his belt.

The burned hole in the carpet was never covered or replaced. Instead, I would find my young self spending hours playing and picking at the melted and charred edges of the burn carpet.

The work ethic instilled into my siblings and I from our Dad is impeccable. You see, we did not get the luxury of sleeping beyond 7:00am any day of the week. We went to school, and when we were out of school, we went to Dad's company to work. When we were not at work or school, we were at church.

We were the sons of Jacob and Annie Malone, and my father spoiled us all. We had the nicest, newest, and even foreign cars before we were all even of legal age to drive. However, he made us work. We would return home covered in grease, grime, and filth after a long day's work while the other neighborhood children played around us. The workdays went from my Dad being in the garages or warehouses instructing us as he did all his employees, to him traveling a lot.

At first, I was relieved when he would take his very regular trips to Corinth or Tupelo, because that meant no more yelling or fear. He spoke harshly to everyone and everyone feared his wrath. Then I realized that the days he would be gone from the company would be days that Jeff was there and left in charge.

Jeff never attempted to bother me at my Dad's company, but the fear crippled me and now there was another male worker who kept referring to me as *pretty*. The door to the men's restroom did not lock, and the worker would always accidentally open the door moments after I entered. So, I began using the ladies' room. My brothers teased me for using the ladies' room, but I did not care. Unable to fathom the idea of a second sexual threat, I knew I had to get myself out of the garage and into the office where my mother worked. There was no way I was going to get out of working, but at least I could work away from those I feared. So, I would spend the next few months intentionally cutting myself, sticking my tiny fingers in flames, learning how to gag myself into vomiting, and becoming an absolute liability and risk to myself and others for me to work in the garage. So eventually it worked, and my Dad sent me to the office to begin learning business management from my mother.

She was fabulous and unbelievably meticulous to detail. She was blunt, uncompromising, and unyielding. She taught me everything that she knew and while I felt safe to no longer be around Jeff or the newest pervert in my life, I thought my Dad would be proud of what I learned in the office.

By the time I was nine years old, I was managing and overseeing inventory and billing for his two businesses. But he was not proud. In fact, he called me weak. He would shout at me that I couldn't do anything a man needed to do. I was just trying to get out of the garage, but he was trying to teach his sons to be what he believed a man to be. By then, I should have been driving the forklifts. To him, I was intentionally running from manhood. My Dad defined masculinity by what he saw in the mirror, and any male different was not a man at all. I felt as if he did not like me.

He became angry with my mother because he believed she was ruining me. In fact, she was my safety. I began defending my mother, but the fights would carry on now in the office. So, while my childhood may have created a business beast in me, I was left damaged to great extremes.

A short while later, the molestation ended. Jeff had now become a father and was really no longer in the picture. While I was relieved from the threat, other threats still existed. I was regularly bullied, picked on, and questioned about my skin complexion and race. I hated being light-skinned; I was told that light skinned blacks only exist as a result rape from white slave masters. I felt as if there was a forever curse on me. I felt as if my skin made me a target. I cannot recall if any sexual references ever occurred towards me from adult women during my childhood, but I do remember that around every corner seemed to be a middle-aged man or so, ready to challenge the limits of indecency.

Because I felt safety and security was not an option for me, I buried myself in my writings. At an early age, I began using writing as my escape from the world around me. I would melt onto the pages as I wrote. Since I was never able to control anything that occurred in my own life, I believe my destiny, my soul, and my future was saved by my ability to control the lives of the characters I created in my works. It was no secret during my childhood that I was obsessed with writing. I could not write my truth, but in my stories little boys were not raped. Women were strong, powerful, courageous, and self-empowered. I wrote the characters I needed to see. I wrote the characters I felt my mother needed to see and I controlled who lived, died, survived, and more. My father would have never allowed my mother to seek counseling, and he was her pastor. Her only outlet for self-help was television, and I was angry that of all the storylines on television nothing related to my mother. Nothing provided a wakeup call to her. So, I decided to write the stories I felt she would need.

Other than the sinful Mrs. Gladden, the remainder of my K-12 education, I was graced with teachers who took time to read every single book, short story, and narrative I placed on their desk after completing my work. Not one teacher discouraged my writings. They were amazed, astonished, impressed, and supportive as to how such a young kid could create such tales of misfortune, misery, and misadventures. Originally, I would become angry and weep at their inability to crack the hidden code in the stories to reveal I was pleading for help. Eventually, I just found peace in the fact that every teacher following Mrs. Gladden, read my works. The science teacher, the math teacher, the band teacher, the choral teacher, they all read. During my middle school years, my parents leased a home directly across the street from the school. Since the school did not have its own gymnasium, the children would have to walk from the school to the parks and recreation gymnasium for P.E. It would be the fall of 1997 when Charles would point out the police cars at my house as we made our way to P.E. The other children all looked as well.

I was not embarrassed, but afraid as to what may have occurred. Following school, I quickly ran across the schoolyard, passed the school sign, and crossed the street into my front yard as I saw Cedric stepping from a car wearing a neck brace. A few moments later, my mother walked out of the house wearing a white uniform shirt with my father's black greasy handprints on her collar. I knew what had occurred. My brother had attempted to protect my mother. My father never harmed his children except for when we stood to protect our mother. My siblings had endured broken teeth, neck braces, bruises, and even guns pointed at them when standing to protect her.

That night, deacons arrived as word began to circulate of the true happenings in the Malone house. We all assured the churchgoers that everything was okay, and that there were no such truths to the rumors spreading around town, as my mother baked lemon pepper pork chops. We would leave that church shortly after as my father prepared to launch his own church. He sat all of his family down, told us the vision he had from God, and gave us all the roles we were to contribute in the new ministry. I became the pianist and choir director; I was twelve.

"Prison ain't no place you ever want to be. Paul and Silas were locked away in prison. Horrible things happen in prison," Proclaimed Rev. Pension. He gave an energetic depiction of the book of Acts during a Sunday school lesson, and concluded with: "Meme, you better not ever go to prison because they gone have your little pretty self. All that pretty yellow skin and pink lips. They'll make you somebody's girlfriend," He stated as I sat on the front pew of my father's new church. There were giggles, laughs, and a few moans, but no one said a word. My parents, the adults, the spiritual leaders, they all said nothing.

By the time I was thirteen, I had begun writing for the local newspaper as a teen writer. My first column depicted spiritual and emotional survival. Today, I wonder how in the hell so many adults missed the obvious clues as to a child in chaos. As I held my $20.00 paycheck in my hand, I waited for my father's approval. He said nothing. Could he believe that I could be more than a mechanic? Would he crack the code in my writings that were now going into 50,000 homes? He said nothing. So, I did all I knew to do. I wrote. I could not stop writing. I was gifted my first typewriter by a substitute teacher. I was gifted my first pack of typing paper by my mathematics teacher. I was experiencing freedom. The checks continued coming as I continued writing. My parents bought my first car, a beautiful navy blue Mercedes Benz. The interior was a peanut butter colored leather, and my brothers had added all the bells and whistles to it. I hated the car because it became another reason for others to hate me. The Malone Brothers were known for their flashy and extravagant vehicles. I was the youngest, and while it made me feel proud that my brothers wanted to add me into their car club, I hated materialism. I hated it all.

Writing expanded into a love of the arts. In a desperate attempt to increase my chances of proving my Dad wrong, I birthed an ambition that would challenge the reality of moral and physical health. I set a goal to learn to play the piano in one weekend. I did so. I set a goal to learn to fully play the trumpet, tuba, saxophone, French horn, xylophone, and organ within two months. I did so. I became known as the unstoppable and creative kid with the greatest ambition ever seen.

Everyone applauded what I was running towards, while I only focused on what I was trying to escape. As my articles became more and more controversial, the telephone would ring as local ministers and community figures attempted to prompt my father to silence my writings about religion, church, and more. To my surprise, he did not. He refused to allow anyone to bully him, so I continued writing.

By the time I was fifteen, I had accomplished every goal I had, and my mind began to drift back into reality. Wrestling with the reality of what I was going home to every evening, led to many outbursts in class. I was instructed to stay after class after I had been a disruption. The small science lab emptied as Mr. Gray sat on the corner of his desk.

"What's gotten into you? You have an F in this class. You know you can't be in all this extracurricular stuff if you fail my class, right? This ain't you," he asked, folding his arms over his big belly. I didn't reply. He shook his head and continued. "You're too good of a kid. You're cute and you have that pretty smile. You're a little bright skinned Ken doll." He waited for me to respond. "You don't look like any of your brothers. They all are darker and look harsh, but not you."

"What's that supposed to mean? They look like what they are supposed to look like. They're black," I snapped back angrily.

"You say that like you're not black," he laughed.

"I'm not black. I'm yellow." I said. His laughing faded as we both realized what words had just fallen from my lips. Where did that come from? I wandered. I had never said that before. I had never thought that before. But in that moment, I realized that I hated the skin I was in.

I didn't know when it occurred, but somewhere along the course of my molestation, abuse, and pain, I had associated all my agony as a function of my skin. If I didn't look like a girl, men wouldn't have touched me. If I looked harsher, my Dad would have been prouder of me. I wasn't the issue. It was the melanin that God withheld from me that subjected me to everything that pained me. The night before, Dewayne had made a phone call to my father informing him that he was being harassed by a group of racist coworkers at the town grocery store. Dewayne, being small in stature, was scared to walk to his car. While we all knew my father only permitted us to work for the family, he reluctantly approved Dewayne's job. However, when Dewayne called in tears, my father rallied his sons together and they left the house. They left me at the house. I had no idea what was occurring until my father and brothers returned to the house with bloody fists and dirty clothes. Later that night the brawl became a laughing matter and I heard my father say that I was not taken because he or my brothers would have mistaken me for one of the white boys.

"You mean yellow like the *Simpsons*?", Mr. Gray laughed again. He noticed I was, becoming angry. "Demetrius, you know that's not a real race, right?"

There was a silence as his daughter who was slightly younger than I was entered the room. She reached into his desk and pulled candy from the desk.

"You in trouble?", she asked me.

"Naw, we're not gonna have any problems. Are we?" Mr. Gray asked.

"I have to go," I stated before walking away. I forced myself to forget my words on my color, and I obsessed over his compliments of my looks. I would spend the next few months trying to reason if his words were decent or indecent. Should I be careful around him proceeding forth? Were his words innocent? I became angry that so much corruption and deceit had plagued my life with suffering, that I could no longer decipher what was normal conversation versus what was criminal. Mr. Gray never spoke to me much following that class. He gave me an A; an undeserved A.

There was nothing challenging me to the degree that it distracted me, so I began to study dance. Suzanna Dish, was the dance teacher hired by my theatre director. Suzanna and I immediately bonded, and she, along with Mr. Ryan, saw endless potential in me. You see, I did not and could not see potential in myself. Our entire lives revolved around the church and what my Dad felt was important. My parents only supported Dowand. They would not attend the concerts, games, events, or performances of the other children. They only supported church services when Dowand preached, and often required the rest of us to skip our own events to be there in support of him also. This would begin the broken and distant relationships among all the children that would carry over into adulthood. My father would accuse the other children of being jealous of Dowand's attention and success. My parents began plotting us all against one another at young ages. Disappointed that my parents were not supporting his rap music goals, Dewayne began to look up to and follow a group of guys in their early twenties who would mentor him musically. The group of seemingly normal guys would take Dewayne to events, shows, and even give him studio time. He was on fire. They were like new big brothers to Dewayne, but they were drug dealers.

So, to develop a life exterior of my church, family, and reality, was amazing. I was not creating art because I believed in art. I created art because I needed something else to focus my pain. The invitation came for our dance group to perform for the then Governor of Alabama and the U.S. Secretary of State. We rehearsed, and rehearsed. To avoid home, I had now sought and won the leadership of many clubs, groups, organizations and more. Anything that I could not win, I founded a competitive organization and lobbied to get all its members to join. It had nothing to do with education, success, or caring for any cause, other than keeping myself from another suicide attempt because by this time both of my parents had attempted suicide as well.

My days would begin at school at 7:00 am, and I would not complete rehearsals and arrive home until almost 10:00 pm. One particular school day following lunch, the younger of the Malone boys were checked out of high school by our oldest brother, Eric. I knew something was wrong. He did not speak what had occurred, instead, he just transported us to the hospital. As I entered Bay 7, I encountered my mother in tears, as her hand was being stitched. She detailed reaching to pull a knife from my father's hands as they fought. My brother Dewayne stood next to me as we were told our father had been arrested.

I had waited 10 years for this moment to occur, and while I always anticipated that I would shed tears of relief, joy, and peace, I did not. Instead, I turned, grabbed my backpack, and walked back to school. I had dance rehearsal.

"Where you going?", Eric asked.

"I'm going back to school. I have practice."

"Man, you need to be here with Mama.", He explained.

"I have a show. I'm sick of this. You're not doing shit with your life anyways. I'm trying to be somebody. I don't have time for this."

I continued walking until I reached the gymnasium. I entered as the many dancers prepared for rehearsal. Everything seemed to be in a fog as I dressed. I had left my queen bleeding in a hospital bed. I was angry with her now. I didn't know why I was angry with her, but I was angry. So, I danced angrily, or passionately some might say. I was applauded as I hid my tears. I gathered my things, exhaled from an exhausting rehearsal and walked home; the sky was dark. I did not know what to expect when I made it home. I wasn't sure if my mother was still hospitalized. I entered the house, and my siblings and most of their girlfriends or wives were present with my mother.

I did not say anything, as I did not know what to say. I entered the back bedroom. Dewayne entered.

"Yella Box, where you been?"

"I had dance practice," I said, still wondering why I was so angry at my mother. I had walked right passed her in the living room. I could not look at her.

"Eric took Daddy's RV to Aunt Brit's house. When he gets out tonight, he's going to live in the RV," Dewayne explained as I packed my clothes. "What you doing?"

"I told y'all I have to go perform in Birmingham tomorrow. Y'all don't listen to shit, and why is he getting out? He cut her!", I shouted.

"She said she reached for the knife."

"So, what? Why the fuck did he even have a knife?", I asked.

"I don't know. I'm just glad he's not coming back here."

That night I attempted to rest. However, I was reminded of the time I pled with my father to give me the pistol he had pulled from beneath his mattress to shoot my uncle. The two men had gotten into an argument and then fought in the front yard, while my cousin and I struggled to break up the fight. My father returned to the house to get a gun as I chased him. Seeing the gun, I cried and begged him not to kill my uncle. He eventually calmed, sat on the corner of the bed, and gave me the gun. I placed it in my mother's underwear drawer. I was ten years old then, and I didn't sleep for months after that.

Here I was now a teen, and his deadly rage had struck again. My mother had been cut. Eventually, I fell asleep. I needed rest for the big performance the next day. I was so happy to be going out of town to perform away from my family. Somewhere near midnight, I was awakened by the sound of a large engine. I knew that sound afar off. I looked from my bedroom window as my father's RV arrived at the corner stop sign. I began to gasp for air. I attempted to wake Dewayne, as my voice seemed to fade away. Within moments the front door opened, and I felt him enter the house.

I trembled and was unsure if I should let it be known that I was awake. I would stay motionless. The bedroom door opened as my Dad's large silhouette appeared in the doorway.

"Boys, get up. Y'all get up and help me get my clothes," he said. We did as directed and helped him remove his clothes from his closet to the RV as the shouting began. I needed to rest. The next day would be my first shot of a big break and freedom. Surely, the U.S. Secretary of State, the Governor, or someone would see me and think I was a talented kid deserving of a big break into show business. I had worked so hard, and I needed an opportunity to get myself out of this house. Something different was happening to me now. I was no longer afraid. I was no longer sad. I was becoming vengeful towards both of my parents and I felt hatred brewing deep down on the inside of me.

How dare they inflict such chaos on the night before the biggest opportunity of my life? I heard her scream as I entered into her bedroom to see him lifting a vacuum to hit her.

"I said *NO!*", I shouted as I pushed him. He fell against the wall as I ran for him. Clamping my hands around his throat, I began choking his large neck. He looked like Jeff. He looked like Mrs. Gladden. He looked like Satan, and I wanted him dead. He lifted me into the air and tossed me through the closet doors. My head was throbbing as Dewayne pulled me from the closet and drug me from the bedroom, out of the house, and through the backyard as my father chased. I didn't know what to do as we were fenced in. I felt my legs collapse beneath me. I heard music as I crumbled in the yard. I couldn't run any further. I grabbed Dewayne's leg for him to save me, not from my father, but from my first nervous breakdown.

By the time my father made it to us, it was clear to him that I had suffered an emotional break. He froze before lifting me and carrying me back into the house. My limbs ached, and I could no longer control my body. I wet myself. He placed me on his bed, turned to the dresser, and reached for a bottle of prescription pills. He flushed them down my throat. The next morning, I attempted to jump from the bed the moment my eyes opened. I was too weak. My body was heavy. I had been drugged. How could I dance? I could barely move.

I looked at the clock. I had missed the first few periods of school, but there were still a few hours remaining before my dance group was to head to Birmingham. As quiet as possible, I stood from my parent's bed, and made my way to my bedroom. I glanced out of my bedroom window. The RV was still parked in the front yard, but my father's truck was gone. I struggled to lift my legs into my pants, but eventually dressed.

I grabbed my belongings and walked to the front of the house to see my mother watching TV.

"I don't feel right. What did he give me?"

"One of his pills to calm you down", she said.

"What kind of pills? I don't feel right." I snapped.

"The doctors say that he's bipolar, so they've put him on a lot of medicines," she explained. I did not know what bi-polar meant. I did not care. "What time you supposed to leave for Birmingham?"

"We leave around four. I need some money". I said.

"Is Laura and Angela going?" She asked. Laura was a dear friend who never let me doubt myself. Her mother Angela had married a childhood friend of my Dad's. My mother felt safe sending me away if Laura and her supportive mother Angela accompanied.

"Yes. I need some money." I replied.

"Call and ask your Daddy."

"I ain't calling him. You didn't get some money from him? You knew I was going out of town?

"I don't feel like dealing with him acting a fool. Now you need to call him and say you are sorry for being disrespectful or you gonna be finding you somewhere else to live," she said without looking at me.

At that moment, I realized my queen had died. She no longer existed. Perhaps, this is why I was so angry. Perhaps, I knew this was coming. So, I did as my mother instructed. I apologized to my father for protecting her because she was not mine to protect. She was his, and I now knew it.

### Emotional Damage

We all carry baggage differently. Some of us carry the baggage in front of us and it can be seen when we are seen. Some of us drag our baggage behind us, and it arrives shortly after we arrive. Some of us even carry baggage on our backs attached to every decision we make in life. We all carry baggage. You don't get to sit in smoky relationships and not smell like smoke. You might not smell the smoke, but those around you smell it.

If you pay close enough attention to people, they will let you know when you smell like emotional smoke. The biggest sign of smelling like emotional smoke is suffocating those you love. Emotionally healthy people have no trouble maintaining boundaries. However, when we have spent so much time in toxic places we melt onto the things or people we feel can relieve our hurts and often suffocate them. You must understand, it's not your love that is suffocating, but your need for the love.

It would become a common practice of my mother to urge children and those who loved her to apologize to my father for standing up against him, even on her behalf. She had begun to practice allowing him to do as he wanted without her response to avoid his wrath. I knew that I had lost her. We had lost her. I knew that I failed. I apologized to my Dad, and he scolded me. As he had always done, he reiterated that Laura, her mother, and none of the people who believed in me cared for me. I said nothing. He instructed my mother to give me money, and I left to board the bus with my crew.

I wanted to distract myself. I needed to distract myself. We arrived at the Jefferson Civic Center, and the venue seemed so large. I was beside myself to think Kimberly and I were the featured dancers preparing to dance for the Governor's Summit. I was honored and mostly because this was an accomplishment that had nothing to do with my last name. No one in the massive building knew or gave a damn about the Malone family, their money, their cars, their companies, their sermons, or their music. This was about me, and it felt damn good. I exhaled and prepared for dress rehearsal. I was nervous, but Kimberly was like a mini burst of energy. She gave me confidence.

We rehearsed the dance once, and then we waited. I assumed there was a technical issue as we were asked to wait backstage. I could see Suzanna and Mr. Ryan speaking. They appeared angry, increasingly angry in fact. I heard Suzanna say, "*FUCK*," and I knew something was wrong.

"What's going on?" I asked Kimberly's mother. She shook her head as if she was in disbelief. I looked at her again. I looked around as everyone in the hall seemed to be looking at me. "What? Are we still going to dance?"

"The governor's wife has a problem with you and my daughter dancing together," she said.

"What? Why?"

"Because this is Alabama, and you're black, and Kim is white." She said shaking her head. I was quiet. I did not know what to say. Should I apologize to the dance crew? Should I apologize to Kim? Should I even apologize to the First lady of Alabama? Perhaps I would have, but I did not know what to do because my first experience of racial discrimination was coming from the most powerful woman in the state. I had always been discriminated against amongst blacks because to some of them, I was not black enough. I was yella, and I didn't know what that meant, but apparently, it meant that I was soft, pretty, too smart, arrogant, or wanted to be white. Even after learning of Alabama's history of racism, it never crossed my mind until that moment that I could experience discrimination based upon the color of my skin from blacks and whites. I was not black enough to be black, and not white enough to be white. I was yella and apparently that qualified me for nothing other than abuse.

"I told them you're not dancing, but when the show starts, you're going up there!", Mr. Ryan said. I nodded. I was terrified.

"And you're going to dance and tell them to kiss your black ass. Then I'll tell them to kiss my white ass." Suzanna said kissing me on my forehead. I hid backstage until it was time for my entrance, and I danced onto the stage.

Shortly after the performance in Birmingham, I opened my eyes to realize all of my siblings had moved out, gotten married while they were still teens, leaving me home alone. I hated them for leaving me there alone. Dowand, Dewayne, and I had never even spent more than one night away from one another, and overnight, they both were gone. They wouldn't visit often and I felt alone, so I began dating a girl who had recently had a child by a man who was much older. It was my opinion that her parents should have had him arrested, she was fourteen, and he was almost thirty. However, I kept my thoughts to myself, for a while anyways. I was a senior in high school, and Nikki and I were engaged. She jumped at the moment to accept my marriage proposal.

It was my opinion that all my brothers used marriage as the escape from my parent's home, and I would do the same. Nikki and I did not argue. We had sex. We had sex everywhere. Here I had spent my entire life hating my skin, my face, and feeling as if no woman would want me, and now a time had come that I could have any woman that I wanted. Nikki knew that I was in a quest to prove myself to myself. We both wanted to be a family more than anything, and while everyone around us urged us to slow things down, we both knew what we were running towards. I had something that was mine. I had someone who loved me, and she would do absolutely anything for me.

We became the popular high school couple. We shared everything. I shared my molestation and she shared hers as well. Her sexual abuse had begun shortly after she turned eight sending her down a path of promiscuity, drugs, and even drug selling. I needed her. She seemed to be sexually aroused as we discussed the perversion we both experienced at the hands of older men. She became intoxicating. I had waited for this escape. At times she would silence after sex and cry. I knew that we were both so damaged. She had witnessed a degree of my father's wrath, and she witnessed my inability to recover. I had witnessed her mother referring to her as a bitch and whore. I was troubled. She was troubled, but we loved one another.

She was more sexually experienced than I was. She informed me of the men, women, couples, and orgies she had experienced since she was nine years old. I did not care. I heard the rumors. My family heard the rumors, but I did not care. I had someone who loved me, and she loved the yella skin I was in. We both had been raped, defiled, and destroyed, and no one had ever given either of us anything, but sex. So, all that we had to give one another was sex. We had school sex, restaurant sex, hospital sex, park sex, and even church sex. It stopped being enough for either of us. We stopped climaxing, and the climaxes became episodes of crying and screaming. She eventually asked me if I would consider the two of us committing suicide together. I was silent. She was silent.

### Damaged Saving Damaged

Silence stiffened me. I wish I could write this and say that I am completely healed in this way, but not quite. You see, the moments in which my parents were silent were the moments I was in absolute agony because I could not gauge what was about to happen next. Would someone scream? Would something break? Would someone leave? Would someone never return?

So, I carried that damage into all of my relationships. I hassled the women nonstop to give me something that I could use to measure how much they loved me or their commitment to not leaving me. As long as we argued, it was fine. I could measure that. But silence moved the earth from beneath my feet because I did not know where silence would lead. I needed some sort of validation. Maybe that came in the act of starting an argument, just so we could makeup and I could be told I was loved. Then I would be at ease. The silent treatment to me was more than the silent treatment. It was the death treatment. It was my slow torturous death.

### The Damage of Identity

It is very important that you understand that not only is the damage of your identity a consequence of a toxic relationship, it is the goal of a toxic relationship. It is no coincidence that you lost yourself.

There was an active, intentional, deliberate conspiracy to convert who you were into who someone else needed you to be.

Have you lost touch with your own goals, passions, and purpose? Remember when you were so full of hope? Do you feel like your dreams have been crushed, and now your purpose is just resting by the wayside? That's a major warning that you've allowed yourself to take the backseat in your relationship. We oftentimes convince ourselves or let others convince us that it is necessary to forfeit what we want for what we think someone else needs in our relationships.

When your identity has been damaged you will find yourself now living an entire life of "what ifs". What if they leave? What will I do? What if they cheat? What if I cheat? What will the kids think if I leave?

Fear is a horrible and heavy name to wear as your identity. Do you find yourself catering to their needs first as opposed to your own? If so, it is only a matter of time before bitterness sets in your heart. You must stop convincing yourself that to follow God, you must constantly martyr yourself to everyone around you. As long as you give, there are some people who will always take.

My need to be a hero always led me to martyr myself for everyone in my life. I believed that there was no greater way to get someone to love you, than by showing them that you will sacrifice it all for them. Like Nikki and all the others, I pursued women who I felt I could rescue from their toxic places. It was a must. My entire masculinity was on the line, and I had to gain back any shred of my manhood that I lost by allowing a man to rape me at five years old. I had to gain back any shred of my manhood that I could by not being able to protect my mother. I was not a man. I had never been a man, and the only way that I could be a man, was with my penis. So, sex became my validation of masculinity.

I rejected Nikki's offer for a double suicide by assuring her that I would build a life for our family. I would finish high school and find an apartment for us as I continued into college. She believed I would protect her. I believed I would protect her. The time came for me to have dinner with her parents to discuss our post high school marriage plans.

"Y'all don't have any plans, money, or anything! What makes you think that y'all ready for marriage?", her father asked from across their large dining room table. Her family was what most southerners called *well-off*, but her parents weren't entrepreneurs as mine were. I liked her father. He was kind, and calm. I thought her mother was cold and brutal. She reminded me of my Dad. Many times, I would see scratches on Nikki's face and arms from fights with her mother. I listened respectfully to Nikki's father as the telephone rang. Her mother answered the phone and stepped away from the table. I knew it was my mother on the call.

"Richard is giving them hell about this marriage stuff," she laughed to my mother. She eventually hung up the phone and returned to the table.

"I may not have a house, apartment, or anything yet, but I'll protect Nikki." I said angrily.

"I'm her Daddy. I protect her. What makes you think you can protect her more than I can?"

"I sure in the hell wouldn't let a damn near 30-year-old man get my 14-year-old daughter pregnant and go free!", I shouted. The room was silent. I did it. I saw it on Nikki's face. I did it. I protected her, and it felt great.

I left her home feeling better about myself than I had ever felt before. I hit the stage the following week in the lead role of 2 sold-out shows, and in my opinion, I performed better than ever. I was strong, I felt invincible.

November 26, 2001 was the day my life changed. A dark night, while on my way to Nikki's house, a masked gunman jumped into my white Cadillac forcing me away from my home and life. While all my friends, family, and town folk gathered at my parent's house praying for my safe return from a seemingly random carjacking, I prepared for what I was sure would become my final curtain call. I was not afraid. I was not afraid to die. I was sure I would die. I was told that I was to be killed. I had been beaten. I prayed, exhaled, and tried to prepare myself. Perhaps I would have been killed, but I heard what the gunman said. I could not make out any other words as I sat bound and blindfolded in the leaves beside my car, but as clear as I had ever heard any words in my life, I heard him say:

"They will pay money for sex with him at least once." The voice echoed. "How much you want to bet?"

Bloody, broken, and bruised, it would be six or so hours later before I would make a narrow escape in the small town of Amory, Mississippi. A caravan of family arrived the next morning to retrieve me and transport me back to Alabama and a hospital where Nikki held my hand as I was treated and questioned by local and federal investigators.

Upon my return home, life would never be the same. The small town of Tuscumbia was hysterical. Counselors had been summoned to my high school to address the frantic state the student body was left in following my abduction. The principal hired a therapist for me to begin visiting once a week, and I was relieved, but the investigation continued as the men had not been arrested or identified. They were still free, and everywhere I looked, people pointed the finger at one another as to who could be secretly responsible.

By this time, most of the Malone Brothers all owned the identical white Cadillacs, and there were rumors circulating that some of my brothers had opted to establish independence away from our father with drug trafficking. I did not believe the rumors, but could it be possible? Was it a case of mistaken identity? Some asked. Was it the white friends of mine who were jealous of my thriving career? My Dad questioned. Was it Nikki's baby's father who knew I was in a pursuit against him? To me, he not only represented her rapist, but mine as well. Even my father had enemies swarming in as dozens upon dozens of vehicles at his garage had recently been spray-painted and vandalized. The FBI began visiting the house regularly, and I began turning down sex with Nikki, as the only thing that now gave me relief was my sleeping pills.

"Demetrius, come in here," my father's voice echoed in the house from his bedroom one morning. I slowly did as instructed. "Close the door." He said. I was nervous. My mother left the room. I began to sweat. I still feared him hurting me. He was quiet. I was not sure what would happen next. He spoke. "The FBI knows you are hiding something. I know you are hiding something, and I told them I think I know what it is." I didn't say anything. He continued. "If it is what I think it is, you have to tell me so I can protect you," he said.

I began to cry. The person I feared, hated, and resented my entire life offered to protect me. I was relieved and hurt at the same time. Would he interpret this offer to help me as a peace offering between us? Should it be a peace offering? He looked as if he would cry also. He gave a big gasp. "Did they do mess with you sexually?", he asked. My heart, my hope, and my head was too heavy to lift. So, I nodded. He exhaled even heavier. "I understand why you wouldn't want anyone to ever find out. I would hide that too if it was me. I wouldn't ever want that out. Go get dressed and go to school. I'll take care of it. Nobody is going to bother you again. I promise you that," he said, and just like that, I never spoke to another investigator again. It all went away. My brothers, my mother, and the investigators never knew the truth.

I walked away feeling loved by my father for the first time in my life. I did not want the public to know I had been sexually assaulted. I was already fighting for any shred of masculinity that I could find. How could I prove to Nikki's father that I could protect his daughter and granddaughter when I couldn't protect myself?

I drove to school in a new car that morning. I looked into the rear-view mirror as my house became smaller and smaller. I then heard the words that he had not spoken and I was no longer relieved. In his efforts to save me, my father unknowingly let me know that what the abductors had done to me was shameful, disgraceful, and that I should choose hiding it over finding and prosecuting them.

I knew then that the truth about a lifetime of sexual abuse and harassment would have to die with me. I felt that such truths would humiliate him. Perhaps he would feel as if he was right and that I would never be a real man. I could never reveal the truth. That morning after twenty-six productions, local awards, national awards, and scholarships, I resigned from performing.

# CHAPTER THREE

## IDENTIFYING THE PERKS

Let's recap. We discussed the many signs that you may be in a toxic relationship, and then we discussed the importance of identifying the damage done as a result of the relationship. Now is a perfect moment to discuss the unspoken perks that keep us coming back to the people, places, and things that cause us harm.

I've kept my end of the bargain and bared my soul to you, so don't hold back on me in this chapter. Your best self needs your current self to be truthful and forthcoming. The truth is that none of us would stay in a relationship that did not serve us in any fashion whatsoever. There may not be monogamy, trust, or love, but deep down your soul is finding something in that relationship that feeds it, be it healthy or unhealthy. You have to figure out what is feeding your seeds of shame. It may be mind-blowing sex, fame, prestige, money, or many other perks. There is something the relationship is giving you that you believe you cannot live without. Oftentimes, we will justify one's toxic behaviors just to reason to ourselves why staying is okay only so you can still have access to that one perk. If it is a healthy perk, then you must learn to administer that perk to yourself and never give that power to anyone. If it is an unhealthy perk, you must get to the root of it and remove it from your soul so that you no longer bargain your self-worth in exchange for it.

You may not know what perk has you addicted to the toxic people in your life, but trust me - they know. They will never tell you until you break up. Then they will use it as a weapon against you. They knew it long ago. They probably practiced getting even better at that perk just because they realize your dependency on the perk.

I want to be clear. There is nothing wrong with a relationship offering one perks. In fact, it is normal and a great thing. However, the problem occurs when the perk is the only thing keeping you in the relationship. You don't stay because of the perks; you stay because of your needs are being reasonably met. The perks are additional.

One of the great things about relationships is that you get to decide your own definition of love. You get to define love for yourself, and no one can challenge, question, or demean your definition.

Learn to ask your partner or spouse what he or she needs to feel loved. Don't assume they need the same thing that you need. If you ask someone of what he or she needs to feel loved, they may answer by stating they need fidelity, support, and loyalty. Others may answer by stating they need financial security and honesty. Some people do not require fidelity to feel loved and secured. There is nothing wrong with either answer. You just have to be in tune with yourself enough to know what your Basic Primary Needs are for feeling loved. Then you have to convey those needs to those desiring to love you.

Most of the time, we cannot explain to ourselves why we define love as we do, so explaining it to others is damn near impossible. They just have to decide if they can meet your definition of love or not. You do not have to explain why your definition of love is your definition of love. How do you know if they can afford your love if you haven't given them the cost? You have to not only give them the price tag to your love but check their emotional credit history. You cannot offer guaranteed emotional credit approval to everyone who wants to be in a relationship with you.

## *Basic Primary Needs*

Prior to entering any new relationship, friendship, job, church, or opportunity you must make a list of your Basic Primary Needs. These are the basics of what you absolutely must obtain from this experience without compromise. You cannot waiver or negotiate on this list. Your list may consist of whatever you need to feel secure and stable, but you must stick to your guns on your Basic Primary Needs. You need to know this list so well that you can decipher in a matter of minutes if someone can meet these needs. Do not adjust your Basic Primary Needs to meet what they are comfortable giving. The truth is that every human on earth has healthy love to give; you just may not be in their emotional budget to receive it.

For this reason, you will encounter people who have the ability to love their children or pets with unyielding compassion and grace but be absolutely vicious towards everyone else. The love is in them, but their children or pets may not require them to get rid of their toxic behaviors the way a spouse or friends would insist upon.

Next, make a list of your Secondary Needs. They are the things that you would like a spouse or opportunity to be working towards or possible. However, this list is only to be observed if the Basic Primary Needs list is first met and secured.

For example, upon entering a new relationship, if your Basic Primary Needs are fidelity, loyalty, and spirituality, then you have to focus on someone who can meet those needs. Do not even turn to the page of your Secondary Needs if he or she is not a viable candidate for your Basic Primary Needs. Your Basic Primary Needs are directly linked to your character, beliefs, and purpose. You cannot compromise on them without compromising on yourself.

If your Secondary Needs are in regard to physical attraction, income, and homes, then you must not confuse this list with your first list. Stand on your list even if others do not agree. You are not responsible for the version of you that others make up in their minds they want you to be.

Let me first advise you to avoid making either of these lists until you seek spiritual, emotional, and mental healing from the toxic places you have been. Too many times in life, we build lives based upon the damaged parts of us. We buy homes, obtain lovers, careers, and even families that the damaged part of us needed to feel whole. Then once we heal, we look around and see a life the damaged version of us obtained, that the healed version cannot use. Most of the time, when we are in toxic relationships, not only are our Basic Primary Needs not being met, but we are sticking around simply because one or two of our Secondary Needs are being met. No jail-keeper is going to rob you of everything. He or she will always find that particular perk they know you cannot live without, and they will excel at providing it.

Following the kidnapping, Nikki and I stopped having sex. Our only language of communicating was now dead, and our relationship began to crumble. I could not bring myself to tell her the truth. Instead, I found myself in a depression and I questioned everything around me. I questioned my friends, my enemies, my parents, my siblings, Nikki, and even God. I did not and could not believe in anything any longer. My high school graduation led to greater resentment towards my parents. My mother knew of my strained relationship with my father and she wanted him to attend my graduation. He refused, but then listed his terms. He promised her that he would attend my graduation if she underwent a lie detector's test to reveal if she had ever been unfaithful to him.

I was furious, but she agreed. The test finally proved the violent accusations we had heard him make against her our entire lives were untrue. He attended the graduation in his anger. He would not believe the results, and he felt deceived into supporting me. I could not continue on this path.

Desperate to find something worth holding on to, I opted to get baptized again. Perhaps, starting back at ground zero would offer me some sense of peace and resolution. I was first baptized at the age of six, and then I went into the water thinking about being molested, and I came from the water anticipating the molestation would stop. This time would be different. I would be in control of what would arise from the water with me. I needed a new start. I had graduated high school and was struggling with PTSD and sleeping pill dependency as I wrestled though my first semester of college. The world seemed cold, very cold. Every season felt like winter. Baptism would be my sweet relief. So, I was baptized for the second time.

Instantly, I did experience a feeling I had never known before. I felt proud of myself. You have to understand the level of spiritual respect the world had for Pastor Malone, his beautiful wife, and his children; so for one of them to come forth and proclaim that I am not as healed as I pretend, that was a big deal. Drying off in the church downstairs bathroom, I looked at myself in the mirror. I smiled. Perhaps, it was just a big deal to me. I dried the water from the concrete floor and stepped into the dark basement. The church was dark. Everyone had obviously left, and I was left there to lock the church. For a moment I was upset, as I expected some sort of fanfare. However, I locked the church and headed to my car where I knew Nikki would be waiting. She would be proud. I opened the car door and sat in the driver's seat as I noticed her skirt was lifted, and her panties were in the cupholder. She leaned the passenger's seat back as far as it would go until it hit the empty child's car seat behind her. I started the engine.

I exited the church parking lot without looking at her. Within moments she began to moan. I continued driving. I arrived at a stoplight. A local deacon from a neighboring church arrived next to me at the stoplight. Assuming I was in the car alone, he blew his horn, smiled, and waved. I did not smile back. Instead, I pulled further beyond the white line. Her moaning increased, and I couldn't take it anymore. I loved her with everything in me, so I did the first thing that came to my mind. I took off my seat belt, put the car in park, and kissed her on her forehead.

I had never kissed that part of her body before. Perhaps, no man had ever kissed that part of her body. As I pulled from her, she stopped moaning and looked into my eyes. I reached beneath me, pulled her hand out of her, lowered her skirt, and returned to my seat. I placed the car in drive. There was silence. With one hand on the wheel and the other hand holding her hand, I drove away.

I realized that my Basic Primary Needs had shifted. I no longer needed sex as I had for so long. I did not want sex. I began working harder to do the things I felt would be pleasing to God. My brothers and I were touring again, and this time we would return to our home of Indianapolis to perform. By this time, Dowand and Dewayne were married, and their wives along with Nikki sang along with us. We were excited to return to Indiana for the concert. I was excited for my family in Indiana to meet my fiancé, Nikki. Being that my parents were still very strict, and we were not married, Nikki and I did not share a hotel room. Before going to sleep the night before the concert, I visited her hotel room. She seemed odd as I closed the door behind me. She sat on the bed.

"I don't want to sing tomorrow," she said without looking at me.

"You're joking, right?", I asked. She didn't respond. "Bae, you know you're the strongest alto I have."

"The other girls can cover it."

"Who? Them? Really? Why are you playing? Do you have any idea how big of a deal this concert is? This is where we come from!", I explained.

"No, this is where you come from. Can't I just sit this one out?", she pleaded.

"No, you can't. How am I going to explain to everyone else why you just decided to bail at the last minute?", I asked, feeling myself getting angry.

"You'll figure it out. You're Demetrius Malone," Nikki mocked.

"What's that supposed to mean?", I asked standing from the bed.

"Look, I'm just saying I can't do it tomorrow. This ain't about the damn concert anyways!", she shouted. "I know what this is really about."

"Tell me what it is really about then," I said, folding my arms.

"You just trying to show me off to your family and everyone that is coming to see y'all tomorrow."

"First, people are coming to see us!"

"No one is coming to see any of y'all wives, and you know it. They are coming to see The Malone Brothers and the women y'all married and to see if we are good enough."

"What are you talking about?"

"Every time we sing people look at us like we are garbage y'all attached yourselves to, and I don't feel like going through that tomorrow. I stand up there trying to act holy and shit and hope your mother is pleased, and it's too much. I ain't perfect. We haven't had sex in damn near a year, and I feel like a whore because I want to have sex with my fiancé. No woman will ever be good enough for you, or for them," she said as she began crying. I took a deep breath.

"Look, I'm sorry. I'm not trying to put pressure on you. I don't know what to do."

"It ain't nothing you can do, I'm already pregnant," she said as the room silenced. Our eyes locked.

"What the fuck did you just say to me?" She refused to respond. "Nikki, don't play with me like that," I laughed. "So, you're like pregnant by the Holy Spirit or something, right?"

"I'm pregnant by Chris Albert," she blurted. A tear fell from her face. She could not look at me. Chris was an ex-boyfriend of hers. I felt ill. I walked to her side of the bed and forced her to look at me. "I'm sorry. I'm pregnant."

Every element of healing I believed I had experienced crumbled before my eyes as she cried uncontrollably. My heart began to race, my palms began to sweat, and I felt my face tingling. "I'm sorry," she repeated over and over. Such an act never entered into my thoughts as a possibility. She was my soul. I felt myself dying, so I did the only thing I knew to do. I stripped my clothes off, pulled her clothes off, and made love to her. "That was all I needed. That was all I needed," she cried as I rested on top of her. I felt her tears racing down my shoulders. I did not speak. I could not speak. I stood from her, dressed, and returned to my room.

I don't remember the concert. It was all a blur, but Nikki did take the stage with us. I did not have much to say to anyone. We loaded the vans to head home, but by this time, my panic attacks were returning with a vengeance. I searched my bags for my anti-depressants or sleeping pills I had been taking since the kidnapping. I realized that I had left the pills at home. While fueling the vans, I fainted onto the gas station parking lot. By the time I woke, we were home.

I woke up the next morning angry. I ignored Nikki's calls. I dressed and went for a drive. Within moments I arrived at an intersection. I froze as my mind drifted. I thought of the painful weekend that had passed. The horn from the car behind me sounded. I looked in the mirror as Chris sat in the driver's seat. Chris was not at all a friend. I put my car in park and walked to him. I could see the nervousness in his eyes.

"We need to talk."

"Bro, I ain't got nothing to say to you."

"She's fucking pregnant!", I shouted. He hesitated.

"Follow me," he said. I returned to my car as he drove. I followed him to his house. He stepped from his car and made his way to the deck on the side of his home. He took a seat. I left my car and joined him. He offered me one of the two drinks from McDonalds. I stared at him. Chris swallowed a mouth full of soda, folded the two bags closed, and spoke. "Man, I'm sorry."

"Fuck you! You have no idea what you've done."

"Man, it ain't that big of a deal. We're all kids."

"No, you are a kid. Nikki and I don't have the option of being fucking kids because we're parents! You're messing with a family! We're a family that I don't want your child to be a part of."

"Dude, she is having a hard time being a part of the Malone family. You act like y'all are the Brady Bunch or some shit, but to everybody else y'all are like a fucking mafia family. That shit scares her."

"If you know so much about my family, then you know that fucking around with me ain't gonna turn out good for you," I raged. There was a silence. I think we were both shocked by my words. Perhaps it was just me. Maybe I was just shocked by my words.

"Here," he said pulling a small cellphone from his pocket. "Read it. She sent me that two nights ago letting me know y'all had sex," he said. I read the text. "She's not pregnant. I already knew she was going to tell you that. She told me she was going to tell you she was pregnant because you can't function or have sex unless you're upset."

"What? You're lying."

"Demetrius, she's not pregnant. Truth is, the girl is crazy about you. She just felt like you were tripping."

"So, y'all decide to fake a fucking pregnancy just so I would break my vow of celibacy? Why fake a pregnancy and lie about having sex with you?" He lowered his head. "Which part is the lie?"

"Just the pregnancy part. We have been having sex. I'm sorry. I promise. I'm sorry," he said as his voice weakened. I did not realize

I had begun to cry until when he offered to get tissue from the bathroom nearest the outside deck.

"I don't need anything from you!", I said, walking away.

"I know her better than you!", he said.

"You, what? Don't nobody know her better than me!", I said looking at him. I felt rage building in me as I clinched my fist as started back up the stairs to the deck.

"Bro, everybody knows but you! Nikki is fucked up! I don't know what you have been through that makes you so blind, but you need to open your eyes. You ain't got no idea how messed up she is," he said. He stopped talking. "I think you need to sit down. You look like you're gonna pass out," he said as another panic attack struck.

"You just stepped in and screwed up God's will. You think you can just screw with God's people, and walk away? I pray He strikes you down for this and I pray He does it today!" I raced to my car. I could not faint at his house. I refused to seem weak. I started my engine and raced home to decay before my mother.

The next time I opened my eyes, I was hospitalized. My body felt heavy. My mother made her way to me.

"You have got to get control of this or you're going to kill yourself," she said as tears filled her eyes.

"I want to be alone," I said, hurting her feelings. She walked to the door as Nikki arrived.

"Hey, Mrs. Malone. How are you doing?", Nikki asked her.

"I'm just worried about my baby and whatever is going on with him," my mother said. I knew that she knew something was not right with Nikki and I. She left.

"Chris told me that you talked to him."

"You're not pregnant."

"No, I just needed to reach you," she said, sitting on the bed. I rested my head on the pillow and looked at the ceiling. I felt angry and confused. The family I was building was crumbling before my eyes. We were less than a month before we planned to marry, and I had to make a decision fast. I unplugged the IV machine, wheeled it behind me, and grabbed Nikki's hand as I led her into the bathroom for sex. Within moments she helped me back into the bed. "God, you really love me, don't you?"

"Why do you even have to ask after all we've been through? I almost died during that kidnapping and I fought to come back to you! This is how you repay me? You fuck Chris?"

"I was only having sex with him so I wouldn't go any further. But I can stop now that we are good. If we're good. I know all of this is my fault, and I'm so sorry."

"You don't have that much power over me. This ain't your fault. I've had these attacks my whole life," I informed her while feeling as if I was lying to myself and her.

"I shouldn't have been there in the first place, or I should have just come outside and said something. I was scared. I didn't know what you would say or do."

"What do you mean? Come outside?"

"This morning when you walked off Chris' deck, I saw when you looked at my car. I saw your walk change. I saw you started stumbling when you noticed my car in the driveway."

"You bitch. I didn't see your car! You were there? You were in the house?"

"He had gone to get breakfast for us. I thought he told you. I thought you knew."

"Do you really think I would have just had sex with you had I known you had just been in his house in his bed again?" I shouted.

"You had sex with me right after I told you I was pregnant by him! So, don't act like I'm crazy," she retaliated.

"Get out. Get the fuck out of my room before I throw you out of that window." She hesitated. I stood from the bed. Nikki grabbed her purse and vanished. I quickly reached for my phone. I had to speak to Chris. I had let him off the hook too easily, and that would not happen again. I dialed and within moments he answered.

"Hello?" He said as he gasped for air.

"She was there? She was in your bed while I was on your porch?" I raged.

"Man, I'm so sorry." He repeated over and over hysterically. Something was wrong as he cried uncontrollably. "God did what you said. He punished my Daddy because of what I did. Man, I'm sorry. I don't understand this church shit! I didn't know," he wept heavily. As I listened, Chris explained that shortly after Nikki left his bed, he entered another bedroom to find his father had died.

I was silent. My rage left. What had I done? I had not harmed his father. I had not harmed Nikki. I had harmed Chris in a way that was much greater than any harm he could have ever done to me. I had used the gift of God to make Chris fear God's powerful wrath against him on my behalf. I had been taught that to harm one of God's followers, was inviting His wrath upon you. That idea had been a scare tactic I had known my entire life, and I believed it to be true. But this could not be God's will, no matter what I had told Chris. Now his father was dead, and Chris could spend the rest of his life feeling as if God's wrath led to his father's death.

I exhaled and began to cry also as I asked Chris if I could pray with him. He agreed. So, I did pray. I prayed a prayer I had never prayed before. I prayed for someone who had harmed me. I no longer prayed that God would destroy those who hurt me, but in that moment, I began to pray for God to heal and help those who had broken my heart. I began to pray for my parents. I had opened the floodgates and I did not care if Chris heard my pleas to God. I fell to my knees on the hospital floor as I held the phone to my ear. I assured Chris that God loved him, and that his father's death was not an act of God's vengeance.

"Amen," I said concluding the prayer. I stood from the hospital floor and returned to the bed.

"And God, please forgive those who touched me when I was a little boy too," he added.

Within moments the call was over. I sat quietly in the bed, as I was astounded. I never knew such a feeling. How was I able to pray for the person I felt destroyed the only thing that meant something to me? My heart was still broken beyond imagination, but there was a new feeling rising from the brokenness of my spirit. It was a feeling of joy. Where did such a power come from? I knew the answer, and at that moment I knew the purpose. I had spent so long avoiding hurt that I never pursued healing. Perhaps my hurt would never leave, but I knew my hurt had a purpose from God. My healing was directly linked to the healing and loving of others. I dialed my father.

"Hello? How you feeling? You need me to come back up there?", he asked all in one breath.

"No, I'm okay."

"Nikki up there?"

"No, it's just me." I said. "Daddy. I think I need to preach. I need to preach. God needs me to preach."

"I've been waiting on you to say it," he said. I was released from the hospital a few days later.

As I embarked on my new journey to stand before a congregation, more revelations regarding Nikki would be revealed by the day. From sex parties during our relationship to sleeping with a relative of mine, I endured the heartbreaking truths. Although we were broken up, I still had not shut her out of my life. The night finally arrived, and I stood to preach my first sermon before hundreds. Following Baptist tradition, the church clerk would present the new minister with a certificate of approval before the large congregation. In walked the new church clerk, Nikki. I was conflicted, uncomfortable, and confused as she reached for the microphone. I couldn't help but wonder what the congregation might be thinking. She gave remarks to excite the congregation before she read the certificate and presented it to me. I embraced her for the first time in months as images of her and Chris filled my mind. She held me longer than I wanted and placed her hand intimately on the back of my head as she held me. She pulled my head closer to her.

"I'm so wet right now." She whispered into my ear. I pulled from her as the congregation applauded. I returned to the pulpit.

By this time, the secret life my fiancé lived was spreading as a blazing fire and there would be no turning back.

"You need to put a stop to this thing with Nikki." My mother said finally addressing the elephant in the room.

"I don't want to hear that. I know what I'm doing."

"You don't know what you are doing! You ain't got no clue what you doing! Now! I mean it!", she said. "I ain't never said anything before, but I meant it. Call it off."

"She is still my family! Just like Daddy is your family! She may not be pregnant, but she sure ain't never hit me or choked the life out of me. You can't tell me nothing about a relationship! Look at yours! I swear God knew what he was doing by not giving you any daughters!" I shouted at her. I had never shouted at her before. Instantly, I regretted my words. The pain in her eyes, I will never forget. I still hate myself today for speaking such words to my mother who once buried a daughter. "I'm sorry." I said as tears filled in my eyes. She spoke.

"I spoke to Nikki's mother and after what she told me she and I both think you need to get away from Nikki. Her own mother said you need to get away from her! How many people have to tell you that before you listen or get yourself killed?", she shouted.

"What did she say?"

"She said she believes Nikki has been lying and that Nikki knows something about the kidnapping." I stood stiff. The room began to spin. I walked away to my bedroom. I looked around. I heard the front door close, and I knew I was alone. A few moments later, Nikki texted me. She was in the driveway to take me to lunch. I gathered the box of her belongings and walked from the house to her car. I sat in the passenger's seat next to her.

"What's that?"

"Who kidnapped me?"

"What?", she laughed. "I don't know. Who?", she laughed again.

"I am not joking!" I said, slamming the box shattering picture frames. Broken glass scattered across the car.

"Why are you asking me that?"

"Your mother told my mother that she thinks you knew something about what happened to me, and you're hiding it. Why would she say that?"

"I don't know. You know my mother hates me! You've seen how she treats me!", she shouted.

"Don't lie to me! Nikki, I've tolerated a lot, but you have to tell me this. I can't go forth not knowing. I can't ignore this rumor like I do all the other ones."

"I don't know what you want me to say."

"I was strangled! I was fucking raped. I was pushed through a fucking window! I got addicted to sleeping pills after that! I want to know the truth! I was on my way to your house that night!" I raged.

She refused to look at me. Instead, she stared out the driver's door into the front yard. She eventually turned to me as tears raced down her face. She could not look me in the eye. I lost myself, and when I found myself, I found myself choking her. She stared into my eyes as tears drained from her face, but she did not fight me. I jumped away from her. Who was I becoming?

That was the last time I ever saw Nikki. Perhaps, I would like to say that I left her because of her many demented deeds, but that would not be my truth. At that time in my life, I had worked towards only one goal, to not be my father. And in the final moment with Nikki, I failed my goal. I became him and I could never forgive myself for that.

Within a matter of days, Nikki and her family quickly vanished from town and a 'for sale' sign was listed outside their home. I rested across the bed in my room as I read the Bible. My mother entered my room.

"You want dinner?"

"No," I said.

"She's gone. I think she is scared you're going to expose her. The phone is ringing off the hook. She's sent messages to people telling them she ended the relationship after you confessed to faking the kidnapping. She's scared. She wants to discredit you, but we don't have to take that." She explained as if she were rallying troops.

"I do not need or want your help. I'm moving out." I said. "I don't care what Nikki says or does. I don't care what y'all say or do. I am tired, and I'm moving out." So, I gave up my sexual perks with Nikki and the financial perks of my family, and I left.

# CHAPTER FOUR

## THE CONVERSATION

Today I regularly find myself discussing toxic relationships with people of all ages from all backgrounds. Whether they're dealing with an abusive spouse or parent, they all experience the same. So, I give the same strategy that I have found to be successful. I wish I could say that I learned this strategy at a young age, but I did not. I did not even learn this strategy following my relationship with Nikki. The strategy I have learned is an accumulation of 36 years of life's difficult experiences.

Let's explore The Conversation. After you have identified the perks you love in the relationship you hate, you have to then have a conversation. But, before you can have the conversation with the toxic person in your life, you must first have a conversation with yourself.

It is of great importance that you come to terms with yourself and face the music of the life you truly have, not the life you want. You have to own your own contribution to the relationship. You have to speak brutal truths to yourself about who you actually share a relationship. You see, many times, we are not actually in love with the person with whom we share a relationship. Instead, we are in love with the person we believe they have the potential to become. We can see them whole, successful, faithful, kind, creative, and loving, even if their reality is nothing like that. So, their 1-day- a- year of proper behavior keeps us enduring toxicity 364 days a year, just waiting on 1 more good day.

You should have by now identified the perks from the relationship, and before you have the conversation with the toxic person in your life, you have work to do. Before you leave a toxic relationship or even a bad job, you must have a plan put in motion. You must have a financial, physical, and spiritual plan in motion for your exit. Remember, the goal is not to leave, but to stay gone. Failing to plan your exit extremely increases the likelihood of returning, or not exiting at all.

If you have identified the perks of the relationships, then you need to now put a plan in motion of how to offer the healthy perks to yourself. You may not be able to give yourself as much as your abuser gave you. If he or she supplied you with $3,000 monthly spending allowance, you may not be able to match that for yourself. You may have to now build a life based on a $300.00 monthly budget. Trust me, three hundred dollars blessed is better than three thousand dollars cursed. You have to find a new living space. You cannot live under the roof with this individual anymore; not because you are addicted to them, but because you are addicted to the perks they give to you. If you cannot afford to move into your own home alone, then find a true friend willing to allow you to sleep on their couch. However, if any way possible, avoid the friends and family members who always spoke poorly of that person anyway. Avoid the people who always made you feel as if it was something wrong with you for being in the relationship. Try to lean on the people in your life who knew how horrible of a situation you were in, but they were patient with your progress and avoided making you feel further damaged with their opinions. You will have to have the conversation with those closest to you as well, asking them to keep your exit private until the exit is complete. You need to let them know that you will be making an exit and what to expect from you.

Then you have to have the conversation with your jail-keeper. You must understand that this conversation is not for them; it is for you. You have to let them know that this is a one -sided conversation. They do not get an opinion or say in this decision. You are simply informing them of your exit and their role in the exit. I do not care if it is family or a spouse. You don't owe anyone a seat in your life. You absolutely must establish clear and precise boundaries. Let it be known that you are leaving this relationship, and the new boundaries he or she is to abide within; whether it is never contacting you again or limiting contact. Whatever boundary you set, you must enforce it because with every line you draw in the sand a narcissistic person will cross it. Stand on that boundary and do not budge.


I moved out of my parent's home shortly after Nikki unleashed her final attack on my life. I told my parents that I could not love myself in the house with them. While I had stopped performing, I was still writing. So, I sold papers to my college peers to make enough money to afford my own apartment. I realized it was time for a new plan. Nikki had been the plan of exit for so long, but now I had to be my own plan. You see, I was the youngest of 5, and all of my siblings left home to get married, so I believed that would be my only escape also. Until that time, I had never considered that I could exit independently, but I did.

With my head held high, I moved into my own apartment. I felt strong. I loved the fact that I had accomplished something no one else in my family had. I expected some of my family to be proud, but they were not. No one visited, and my father felt betrayed. I would further my education, begin working in social work, purchase a new car, and build a great life. But, it was still a lonely life. I filled my life with more church than God, but I did not understand or know that there was a difference. I was nearing two years without sex, and I was not at all tempted. I spent seven days a week in church. Rev. Campbell, and his family were new to our church, and with him came almost ten children. I served as youth minister, and I took the job seriously. I loved the many children. Rev. Campbell was nice. His wife was nicer, but she was almost forty years older than he was. Her children were his age, and her grandchildren were the age of his biological daughter. It was so many of them, but the kids loved the youth ministry. I made sure the youth ministry loved them. I avoided Rev. Campbell most of the time as he always appeared to be in competition with the other ministers to be my father's favorite. Nonetheless, I loved the ministry.

It was my entire life, but the rules and regulations of religion left me cold and judgmental of so many. Holidays were especially miserable as all my siblings would leave the family home to join their own individual families. I would return to my home alone. By 2006, I had decided to return to perform after many years, so I wrote a new stage play. This time I would write a Christian based comedy - drama. Unfortunately, the fire that was once attached to my professional name had died, so I struggled to find sponsors. Determined, I opted to just pay for the show myself. Production began, but I struggled in every way.

I had dedicated so much of my life to my father's church, that taking time to produce and rehearse the show led to me being regularly scolded. I was told I was putting the show before God. I was subjected to regular rebukes from my father and even Rev. Campbell, informing me that I was going astray, and I was sinning against God for missing church events to work on the production.

I began to fear they were right, and that I would fail because God was not with me. However, something at the core of who I was knew I had to proceed. I believed that there was much more in me to give the world, and my father's church restricted me from doing so. I was becoming increasingly concerned about those who would never enter a sanctuary, and I wanted to reach those people.

While producing the show, I saw Tonya. I had known Tonya since I was a young child. Her parents were friends with my parents when we were children.

I knew that she had a child, and at first, I was reluctant after not only losing Nikki, but her daughter as well. However, I made my move, and Tonya and I began dating. She was a few years older than I was, and for all visual purposes, she was the exact female version of myself. She even came from a popular musical family as well. It seemed perfect; I fell in love fast, despite my trust issues. As I began to practice transparency, I informed Tonya of my trust issues. Things were brilliant, more than brilliant. Things were indeed perfect, and at twenty-six, I fell more in love with Tonya as I ever knew possible.

Desperate not to lose this relationship due to sex, we avoided sex. You should have seen how people celebrated such a beautiful couple. Many were happy to see me just move on from Nikki. However, my mother's sisters were not at all happy about my newest relationship. They reminded me that Tonya had dated a close relative of mine before. I knew it, but I wrote it off in my mind as teenaged puppy love.

In the sixth month of my new fairy tale, I purchased an engagement ring. *Lord, Save My Family* had opened and broken box office records. My pockets were stuffed, and I felt like I was on top of the world. I was making a fierce comeback. Suddenly, our relationship halted as Tonya informed me that she needed time alone. I knew that something was occurring in her life, but she was secretive. I feared another man. She informed me that a family matter required her emotional and spiritual focus and that she could no longer contribute to our relationship. She told me to give her time. So, I patiently waited and placed the ring beneath my mattress.

It would be during The Malone Brothers 20th Anniversary Celebration, that I learned Tonya was dating another man. I was furious. I saw Rev. Campbell enter with his army of children. I knew he would voice his judgmental opinion to me of Tonya, as he did (he waited on moments to correct others). Tonya would begin to bring her new boyfriend to concerts with her; when she did, as the usual crowds, musicians, (and more) all would question me. This would become a toxic back and forth that would last a couple of years. I refused to allow another woman to damage me. So, I decided I would visit a church I knew she was visiting. Following the service, I would take her out to dinner and completely put an end to the on again and off - again relationship.

I arrived at the small country church. I felt as if I was walking in the church from the movie *The Color Purple*. Tonya's aunt was the guest preacher; I thought she was very nice, pretty, and a hell of a singer. Tonya's mother and her aunts were the inspiration of the Malone Brothers singing. As kids, we mimicked them in all our performances. We sang all their songs, and even copied some of their choreography. However, I ignored every song, scripture, prayer, and even the sermon. Truthfully, I wasn't there for worship. I was there to meet with her and have the conversation. But there was no plan. I would just let her know that I was done. As the conclusion of the service neared, a short lady with messy hair and a flower dress approached the altar. Her hands waved in the air as she began to speak prophecies over everyone in the front of the church. Coming from my traditional Baptist background, I had never seen anything like this. I had never heard of anything like this, but it was magical, and Minister Gloria had my fullest attention. She would speak of secret and private matters, and the weeping congregants would confirm. She would then detail God's plan or desire for their next blessing.

I watched her speak things to a few individuals that I knew. I knew that she was accurate. What was happening? People began racing to Minister Gloria. Then she saw Tonya's face. It seemed as if the sea of people parted in the small church as she made her way to Tonya. Tell her to 'stop acting a damn fool', I wished Minister Gloria would say. Instead, she addressed Tonya's hurt, disappointment, and inability to love. Tonya cried. She did not say what I expected, but it did make me feel great to hear her tell Tonya that God loved her. The service ended, and I waited at the rear of the sanctuary as Tonya made her way.

"Let's grab a bite to eat. We need to talk," I said.

"I rode with my family. I think we're going out to eat."

"We need to talk," I said, more firmly.

"That's him," a voice said. Tonya stepped aside as Minister Gloria stood behind her. "This is the man God says is your husband." We stood speechless. She continued, "Love him. You love her." She looked at me. "Let me talk to you," she said, wrapping her arm around mine and escorting away. "Every demon on this earth is trying to get you to leave that woman. You're tired, you're hurt, and you want out. That woman right there is your destiny, and if you leave her you leave your destiny. Don't listen to the devil. Marry that woman," she said, squeezing my hands. I nodded. I nodded again.

Destiny? I had a destiny. I looked at Tonya. I grabbed her hand and we drove to dinner where I proposed. She declined again and informed me she was seeing another man. I wasn't angry, I wasn't upset. I believed it was the prophecy fulfilling itself. I stood strong. I went home and went on with my life.

I began to be in agony. I had conditioned myself to leave hurtful places, and now God wanted me to stay in this place? God was my everything, and all that I had. So, to refuse God's will was something I could not do. So, I let her come and go, and go and come for years until I could not endure anymore. Arguing on the telephone again I ended the relationship with Tonya as I drove nearly slamming into a small blue sedan in front of me. The beautiful woman blew her horn, hoping I would get off the phone.

As I neared the red light next to her, I rolled down my window to apologize. I would say I'm sorry for being careless, but when my mouth opened, I asked her to dinner. She agreed. The next six months of my life, I spent in love with Tonya while Adrianna was in love with me, and I mean she loved the hell out of me.

I let Tonya know that I was in a new relationship, and she seemed upset, but we both knew I would drop Adrianna at any moment for Tonya. I was nearing the sequel of *Lord, Save My Family,* and expecting an even larger profit than the original. I wanted to love Adrianna. I so desperately wanted to love her. I did not know how to lie, so I told her that I still loved Tonya. She told me that she was aware, but she was willing to be with me until I could love her as she loved me. She was so unbelievably kind and loving. I broke my vow of celibacy with Adrianna. I did not feel as if I was cheating on Tonya, I felt as if I was cheating on God. So, while Adrianna slept in my bed, I crept onto my balcony overlooking the dark city.

"Hello?" Minister Gloria answered. I had begun regularly calling her for spiritual guidance.

"Hello. I hope I didn't wake you."

"No, I'm awake. Just reading the word of God. You staying on the path, baby?"

"I don't know. I mean, there's this other girl…"

"Umm mmmm. No. baby. Satan comes in many forms. Don't you let that devil in your bed. It don't matter what you wanna doing. You're the man. The head. God is holding you accountable."

"Yes, ma'am," I said feeling hopeless,

"You love Tonya don't you, baby?"

"Yes ma'am, but I don't want this anymore. I don't want to be with Tonya."

"You think Mary wanted to be pregnant as a little virgin girl? You sold out to the Most High. It ain't about what you want. It's His will."

I ended the call and returned to the bedroom. Adrianna snored horribly, but I didn't care. I hated myself because I knew I was about to break her heart. Her rapist had been out of prison a little over a year, and she shared a child with him. I think she still cared for him also, but she found peace in believing a loving man like me could love her. But I wasn't a good man. I did good things for good reasons, but I wasn't a good man. I decided I would give Adrianna a try. The next morning Tonya called to tell me that she loved me and wanted us to be together. And like that, I broke Adrianna's heart. I returned to Tonya. The reunion would last but a few days before Tonya would end the relationship again. I found myself with Adrianna once again. She was the most peaceful woman I had ever known. She was perfect in every way. I just could not love her as she loved me, and I couldn't justify to myself why that was okay. So again, I broke Adrianna's heart as Tonya groveled back to me. I knew that Adrianna hated me now, and while I hated myself for hurting her, Tonya and I had reached a new place. It seemed right. So, we reunited days before the new production opened to even larger audiences. From the stage, I saw Adrianna's face. I hoped she would be happy for me. The next week, after five years, I proposed to Tonya again. She accepted.

Every dream I had was now coming true. I had relaunched my career, I was successful, and we were on the road to matrimony. I called my parents to inform them of the engagement. They were furious. My father's wrath showed it's head again. He was furious that I had made such a move without consulting him, and that someone else had informed them of the engagement before me. My parents boycotted the engagement and the wedding. My relationship with my mother began to crumble. Aside from running my production company, and working as a social worker, I was running my mother's child development center. She would not speak to me. I stood outside her office door during an early morning to hear her phone conversation with her sister.

"If Tonya left him again, I wouldn't be surprised if he killed himself. He just as stupid now as he was with Nikki." Her words cut deeply. They made me feel unhealed. Perhaps, because they were true. But because of her life choices, I felt she had no grounds to judge me. As I walked to the front office in walked Rev. Campbell.

"I hear you and Tonya getting married."

"Yes, we are."

"You need to apologize to your Daddy for the way you did this. You been out of line for a long time; all these stories and plays. God ain't pleased with all this devilish stuff you're doing. You know you ain't ready to get married. Marriage is a serious thing," he said, leaning over my desk. Those words still ring in my ears today. That was the last time I saw Rev. Campbell.

The next morning, I woke up to phone calls and texts urging me to turn on the news. Rev. Campbell had been arrested for the rape and molestation of his daughter and several of the grandchildren of his wife. The molestation had gone on for many years, and it was likely that his wife was aware. My heart broke for the many children, many of which were mentally disabled. My father called a meeting at the church for the entire congregation to discuss the recent arrest and our process to remove Rev. Campbell from his affiliation with the church.

The children were innocent and young. But I listened, and I watched for months as the children became the blame and target from so many. I was crushed. I felt as if I failed them as their youth pastor. How did I miss the signs? I had experienced the same thing. How did I become so self-involved that I had such evil occurring under my nose, and I saw nothing? I blamed myself. Perhaps, had I not been focused on launching my production company, I would have noticed the molestation occurring right under my nose.

Following another successful show and guilt, I put my focus on my quest to be of greater service to the unchurched people in the world. Eventually, I made the decision no Malone had ever made. I told my father that I was leaving his church, and I would begin doing ministry on my own. He did not want me to leave the church, so he offered for me to become pastor. I declined. The next morning, I informed him that I would launch my own ministry. A few hours later I learned my father had resigned as pastor and placed Dowand as the new senior pastor. I supported Dowand, but I knew my father's heart. He knew of the significant role I played at his church, and he feared the congregation would leave the church to follow me. While he felt he could not compete, he felt Dowand could. Instead, I told no one at my father's church of my new vision. My vision from God was simple. I was to simply reach out to the people who are statistically less likely to ever visit a church and offer them God. But my family blackballed me.

My parents accused me of trying to destroy everything they built, and they called all of the clergy in town to ensure no one offered support of my efforts. I began to find comfort in my older brother Cedric and his family. Cedric had distanced his household from the rest of the family years before. While he lived in the same city as most of the family, no one knew where he lived, and he avoided all contact. Years would pass without any interaction, but I always understood his choice to distance himself and his family from the rest of the family. He wanted to live a peaceful, healthy, and emotionally stable life void of spiritual manipulation. I needed to know how to do the same thing, so I found strength in him.

I cried, but I continued. I knew that God had a plan for my life. I did not know everything about God, but I did know that God was love. So, I would simply let people know that they were loved. Within a matter of months, I began walking the streets in Sheffield, Alabama, where I was also a business owner. I had never been in the projects, but I wanted to meet people. Before long, the city council offered a recreation center for services and classes. I proceeded with an elite team as we worked diligently for the spiritual, social, and economical enhancement of an impoverished community. I prepared to welcome Tonya and her daughter into my home, but she refused to leave the city with her family. Blinded by love, I walked away from my home, 3 jobs, and everything stable in my life. I moved to be with her in Decatur.

I settled into our new brownstone a while before the highly opposed wedding. My money was running out fast. Surely, with my credentials, I could secure a new job in Decatur to supplement an income until the newest show premiered. There I was in the prime of my life - young, successful, and very financially stable, but I still wanted the exit I believed my brothers made to finally heal from our childhoods. I believed that the ultimate healing from what I experienced as a child was to create the polar opposite. No dream, home, career, or bank account could give me that.

I knew my father would not officiate the wedding he despised, so we asked her father to read a scripture while my father prayed. My brother Dowand would officiate. My best man Ricky and I stood in the small office right of the pulpit as guests filled the sanctuary. We were both quiet. He knew I loved her, I knew I loved her and I was about to make all of my dreams come true. I felt a vibrating in my pocket. I pulled the new phone I had recently purchased from the tuxedo pocket. I read the text. This was not my phone, it was Tonya's phone, and I was reading the reply from the man she had just told she truly loved him. She had asked him to stop the wedding or she would marry me thinking of him. My hand trembled as I held the phone. This was the conversation she had engaged in the hour before our wedding. My heart raced.

"What? What's wrong?", Ricky asked. I couldn't speak as the music increased. I looked at him as the usher opened the door.

"It's time. Let's go," the usher smiled. I gasped for air and began to cry. I folded the phone into my pocket and made my way to the altar.

# CHAPTER FIVE

## EMBRACE THE PAIN

Tonya and I slept in separate bedrooms the many months following our wedding. The nights were filled with arguments and rage as I pleaded with her and demanded she cut off all communication with the man she truly loved. She refused but eventually agreed after I began to blackmail her. I threatened to expose the texts to the public. Everything was horrible. I had no peace in this town, and I hated myself for betraying myself in such a way. The truth is that I would have never exposed the truth to anyone because I would also expose how weak I was. Everyone already knew I was weak. My father's prayer during the ceremony included words pleading that God would enable Tonya to accept Demetrius and love him.

My parents refused to join us at the reception. They along with others from their church chose to dine at a restaurant instead. As the program called for Tonya to dance with her father while I danced with my mother, I felt hollow. But like many other times, Elease showed up for me. Joining me on the dance floor at eighty-six years old, was my mother's mother. My beautiful grandmother put my hands on her hip, swayed and made me smile. I did not think I could smile on my wedding day.

"You have to learn what is best for you. I know why you're doing what you're doing. None of my children wanted to see you marry Tonya. They hate it."

"What about you?" I asked wondering if she knew her opinion meant the world to me.

"I know what you are running from. I ain't gonna judge you because I know what you're running from. You ain't gone be running always, Meme. God has good things in store for you. He has things that are bigger than your mama, your daddy and even Tonya. You just keep praying," she said into my ear as we danced.

I think it is important that you understand that often when you experience such horrific pain at an early age, you lose your ability to tolerate pain as you enter adulthood. So, you make poor decisions all in efforts to avoid pain. As I read the text messages that pierced my soul in an instant, I made a decision that marrying a woman that loved another man would be less painful than the hurt already boiling on the inside of me from years of abuse and neglect.

It is utterly irrelevant to go through the first four steps of leaving toxic relationships if the fear of pain paralyzes you from taking your exit. You must realize that fear and God do not and cannot occupy the same space. Most of the time getting better hurts. Many people live their entire lives at their bottom potential because their upper potential requires pain. I was tired of the depression and anxiety attacks. I could not endure that pain anymore. I married a woman I knew did not love me. But, perhaps this too was a part of what Minister Gloria anticipated. She attended the wedding and applauded proudly as if she was one of our parents.

I believed that if ever there was a marriage that God would restore, it was mine. We both loved God, but the marriage was horrible. We had sex three times the first year of our marriage. The third time, she became pregnant. I was excited about the baby, as was Tonya, but we were not ready. We had moved back to Tuscumbia where my family was so that I could find work and continue my ministry in Sheffield. By this time, the current mayor and the former mayor were preparing for an electoral run-off and the district I served would be the district to influence the election. Together, both candidates requested I join them for a meeting. They informed me that I had become the most influential person in the city, and they wanted me to invite District 4 to my center while I moderated a debate between the two of them. While I favored one candidate myself, I informed them both that I would be unbiased, and I would bring the city together for the debate and forum.

At twenty-three years old, I moderated the massive event that exchanged heated debates on police brutality, waste management, and many other great concerns. Tonya sat at a table in the back of the room. She seemed to be proud as she assisted with the many attendees. However, everyone was not proud. By the time the debate made the news and my involvement was known, anonymous phone calls harassing the city officials, supporters, and many more began. I was being accused of ridiculous lies, none of which anyone believed, but the threats and demands to cut ties with me were so vicious, most walked away. I knew that my family was responsible. The attacks were immediate relatives, or distant relatives, but I knew the work of my family.

Tonya and her family hated her being away from them, so she was using the few dollars we did have to travel back to Decatur almost daily to see her family. I felt as if I would go mad. My household was under attack from my family, and my wife was seeking a reason to return to her family anyway.

Learning of conversations and interactions with other men was a painful norm by this time. We would argue, and I would want to do the same - but I could not. I had resumed management at my mother's company. The company began to struggle, and my mother was planning to close the business and retire. I was frantic as to what my next move would be. We welcomed an absolutely beautiful baby girl into our lives, alongside of Chelsey and Nicholas. But Tonya, and her family were raging towards me. Tonya wanted to move back home and live with her mother the first few months with the new baby, and her family was angry that I refused to allow my family to leave me. I knew that our marriage could not survive such a thing. Besides, she was thirty and had already been a mother for ten years.

So, Tonya threatened me. Due to the crumbling business, my mother's company was unable to pay me on time. We were facing horrible hardships and Tonya informed me that if we lost our home, she was taking the kids back to her mother's house. I could not lose them. As payday arrived, I waited for my parents to pay me. Instead, my father used the entire payroll to purchase land in the countryside where he was born. I lost everything. Tonya took the children and left for Decatur.

Being angry with my parents, I refused contact with them for weeks. I ignored their calls as they had once again afflicted my greatest fears on me. I had to figure out a way to save my family. I broke into my mother's office and stole a check from her checkbook. I wrote a check to a new landlord for slightly less than the amount of payroll I was due. I raced to tell Tonya, I had a new home for us, and she did not have to leave me. She sat in our SUV as I packed and moved everything to our new home.

My mother called and assuming she had learned of the check, I answered without apology. I was tired of being bullied and ran over. Instead, she asked me to come over to help her move an oven. I declined angrily and hung-up.

"She's in emergency surgery. It's touch and go right now. All we can do is hope for the best," the doctor said standing before the Malone family in the surgery waiting room. My mother had ruptured her spleen attempting to move the oven on her own. I felt horrible. What had become of my relationship with the woman that was once my queen? I once defended her with my life, now she was on the brink of death because of my rage and anger. I hated myself and prayed for God to save her. She narrowly survived, but by the time we made it home, the new landlord informed me that the check was declined for insufficient funds and I had one day to vacate the home before he had me arrested. Exhausted and drained, Tonya sat in our SUV as I moved everything from the home to a storage.

We slept at my parents' home for weeks as I aided in my mother's recovery. I felt as if I could not ask Tonya to end the conversations with other men because of my failures, so I stopped complaining. I would just swallow the hurt. I picked up work as a social worker again as the cold winter came. Tonya hated me. I knew it. I hated myself, but I loved the children. A few weeks after my mother arrived home from the hospital, I left the family home to visit a new client. I had begun counseling a young boy who had been raped by his grandfather. I drove up the icy mountain to the small ragged trailer.

I sat in disgust as the boy's mother seemed to believe the grandfather was treated unfairly. After a few hours, I left the home and started down the mountain, but made a wrong turn. I prepared to turn around, when a cold chill crossed my neck. I recognized the road. I continued further as I realized this was the road I was forced onto during the kidnapping, where I was first tied and placed into the back of the car. Overcome with pain and anxiety, I lost my breath, I lost my mind, and I lost control of the car as I drove across black ice. Within moments I opened my eyes on the wet, icy ground at the bottom of the mountain.

My mangled car rested not far from me. I could not move. I could not see how far over the mountain I had crashed, but it was far. An hour passed as I drifted in and out of consciousness. I could feel my eyes closing every time I would blackout, and it was my hope and greatest prayer that God would relieve me at that moment. After all I had survived, a car accident would be my death.

"His neck is broken," I heard from muffled voices. I felt cold hands on my body. I heard a helicopter over me. Certain I was dying;

I could hear my grandmother's voice in my head. Was it possible that there was more to me than what I had seen and where I had been? If I survived this, would I survive for more pain and misery? I spent my entire life being told and showed that I was not enough. I could not endure the pain further. God thought otherwise as twelve hours later with doctor's scratching their heads, I walked from the hospital. I walked in pain and walked in tears. I walked back to a car that would drive to a home that was not mine. There had always been pain in my life, but at that moment, I realized when the pain became unbearable. It was always at the times in which I stopped writing that I lost myself in my pain. So, while pain is inevitable, I had to return to the only pain medicine that had saved me since I was that five-year-old boy being violated.

We moved to Decatur, and I dug through my old boxes to find *Diamonds*. *Diamonds* was the stage play I wrote 10 years before, following being drugged by my father. The story chronicled the lives of a wealthy African American family and the abusive patriarch that dominated the lives of his children. I never produced the show. It was never supposed to see the stage. It, like many of my earliest works, were just written as my private pain medicine. But I was tired of carrying hurt alone. My hurt had to have some purpose behind it. What would become of my family if I produced the show to my massive fan base? Would the supporters and my family connect the story to the myths of the Malone family? I did not care. I was broke. I needed a job, and if there was anything I knew how to do: I knew how to write and perform. I needed healing, so every area of my life pointed to

*Diamonds*. So, I embraced every bit of hurt I would endure from the production, and the journey began.

# CHAPTER SIX

## WHAT TO DO WITH THE DOWNTIME

During my years in social work, I also taught drug and alcohol relapse prevention. I worked diligently to detail to my clients the importance of filling their downtime with constructive and meaningful practices. I will share that same importance with you. You, just like every other person on this earth, are addicted to something. One night I woke up in the middle of the night. I made my way down the stairs to the kitchen for something to drink. Without turning on any lights, I kept through the house before tripping over a stroller. As I began falling, my hands immediately began reaching out for something – anything - to grab that would prevent me from falling. It was a natural reflex, I didn't think about it. It was just my mind and body's way of trying to protect me by seeking something I could cast all my weight upon to save myself from being hurt.

I felt my hands grab hold of an ugly chair Tonya had purchased. I hated the chair, but it saved me from falling. After that, the chair wasn't so bad. You see, that is how addiction works in each of us. Life has a way of knocking each of us off of our feet, sending us hurling into pain. It is our natural instinct to reach out for something to prevent us from falling. How can we judge the man who grabbed hold of cocaine as he fell, or the woman who grabbed hold of promiscuity as she fell? The fact is no one has ever grabbed hold of any addiction that does not serve them. The difficult part of life is trying to convince someone that embracing the pain is better than embracing the perk that shields the pain.

Once you've left the toxic place or relationship in your life, you have got to find something else to devote your energy. While I had not yet made my full exodus, I was having revelations that gave me signs change was coming. *Diamonds* was absolutely massive. Every performance sold out. I even cast Tonya in the show, she was fabulous. And while we worked well together, her obsession with money and men still concerned me. She was flirtatious with everyone, but I did not think she would actually have sex with anyone else. She informed me that she just loved having the attention of other men.

Following the opening weekend of *Diamonds*, we visited my parents. My heart raced. To my shock, they were astounded and pleased with the show. My father sang its praises and compared the show to the 1980's TV show *Dallas*.

"Y'all are on your way," he assured us. The tour across the south began shortly thereafter, but not all reviews were positive. I had been known as a conservative Baptist preacher and pastor for years, and I had just baited my Christian audience into a non-Christian themed drama filled with violence, sex, corruption, and abuse. There came religion again. I lost sponsors who had partnered with me for years, but I did not care. I had presented the image of Christianity on stage that people wanted to see for years and it was fake. Life was messy and painful, and *Diamonds* was my truth.

Demetrius Malone Productions that originated with just me was now over twenty people traveling by a caravan of cars, bus and moving trucks. I felt liberated. As the tour landed us in Tupelo, Mississippi, I visited a local radio station for a promotional interview. Feeling on top of the world, I felt invincible. The radio DJ suddenly asked me was I aware that I was but a few miles from the location I escaped during the kidnapping. I froze. Not only did I not know how to respond, I realized that almost ten years had passed, and I could not remember the last time I thought of the kidnapping. Tonya looked at me, as she knew I was uncomfortable.

I acknowledged the question simply and ended the interview. After the tour wrapped, things quickly settled back to normal. I wanted to focus more on myself and my family, so I stopped performing with my brothers. The arguments began again. Tonya's family felt as if I was a bum and no work ethic. I did not care what they thought, but I did care what she thought.

Immediately, I began writing the sequel to *Diamonds*. A sunny Monday morning, Tonya and I woke up early. She rested in the bed with baby Alaura as I made a run for breakfast. Before getting a mile from the house, Tonya called me screaming.

"Help! Someone is kicking the door in!"

"What?"

"They're coming in the house!", she screamed as I heard the loud crash. I quickly turned the car in a circle in the middle of traffic and raced towards my home as I dialed 911 on a separate cell phone. "He just ran out the kitchen door. He's getting in a gold car." Tonya cried. I made it to my street to see the car running through a stop sign.

I described the occurrence to the 911 dispatcher as I sped to chase the fleeing vehicle.

"Don't chase them." Tonya shouted as did the dispatcher. I hung up both phones as I increased speed. For ten years, I lived in fear that the monsters who kidnapped me would one day resurrect themselves and come after my family. In my mind, this was that day, and one of us would die this day. There would be no more fear. It would be peace or death. I thought as I neared the car fleeing me. I followed the car into an apartment complex, and out jumped a man who vanished between the many buildings. The woman driving the car quickly opened her door to run. I grabbed her and slammed her against the car. She screamed as I shouted at her. I held her face.

"Please! I'm sorry! I'm sorry. My son!", She cried, attempting to breathe. I looked into the car to see the toddler thrown in the floor of the car by the reckless driving.

"You bitch. You do this with a kid in the car?" I opened the back door and pulled the screaming child into my arms. She reached for him. "You will never touch this child again, and if you touch me; he will watch his Mama die today."

"He is my son."

"My daughter was in my house!", I raged as an army of policemen raced towards us. Abigail eventually gave the name of her coconspirator.

"She's going downtown, and social services is taking the kid. You should go home and check on your wife and kids," the heavy detective advised.

"What about the guy? He got away."

"She gave us a name. We'll check it out, but it looks like it was just a regular attempted robbery."

"You can tell that just by talking to her? What's his name?"

"Mr. Malone, I understand you're upset, but I've been doing this a long time. It was just a normal robbery."

"I'm not just a normal person, so I can't accept that was just a normal home invasion."

"You need to calm down. Now, you defied the dispatcher, and you could have caused endless number of casualties with that chase. You could have killed that girl," he said.

"I would have killed her- not could," I said.

"I'm trying to be patient. Just go back to your car. It's over"

"Over? You expect me to go back to my family and tell them that the man who just invaded our home on them is still on the loose? You expect me to let them live in that type of fear? I've dealt with that shit for ten years. They're not going to go through that. You have twenty-four hours to find him, or I will."

"Do you know I could arrest you for talking to me like that?", he said, angrily.

"Demetrius let's go. You need to see about Tonya and the baby," Tonya's grandmother said from her car. By the time I made it home, Tonya and already packed clothes. She and the girls moved in with her mother, again. I desperately needed my family to know I could and would protect them, so I stayed in the home alone that night. Afraid myself, I wanted to show them the threat was over. Nothing worked. She refused to come home. The next day every local news station identified the man who invaded my home. He had a Biblical name, King Solomon. He had not been arrested, and I was out of patience. I did not have my family, so I had nothing. I knew that Tonya was terrified, but 90% of our marriage was spent with me trying to convince her to spend time with me in our home versus camping out at her mother's home every day. I was afraid she would never come home. The detective called me.

"Mr. Malone, I'm checking in on your family," he said.

"Did you find the man who broke into my house?", I asked.

"Mr. Malone, I was concerned about you. I know who you are. I ran some things and I know who you are. I know what happened to you when you were young. This ain't the same thing. You need to understand that," he explained to no avail. I became angrier that he had used his time to search my past instead of the man who invaded my home.

I immediately searched Facebook for King Solomon, and eventually found him under an alias. I created a fake profile picture of an average looking black woman. I began to engage in conversation with him. After a week or so, he returned communication, and the hunt began. As I proceeded as a fictitious woman, he expressed interest. It would not be long before he would ask for money. I told him that I could bring him the money. He asked for a phone number so he could call me. I had not anticipated this, but I was close. As Tonya stopped by the house for more clothes, I informed her of why I had been so preoccupied. She was sickened by my pursuit to catch King Solomon.

She even questioned my sexuality for the messages written to lure him. We argued and she told me she did not want to be married to a man who could have such conversations with another man, even if I was pretending to be a woman. I was furious, but she would not stop me. My family was afraid to take showers alone. I would not rest until I found him and they had peace.

I phoned Katie, who was one of the new talented actresses in *Diamonds*. I explained what had occurred and that I needed her help. I offered to pay her, but she refused pay. She wanted to assist in catching King Solomon. Katie agreed and assumed the voice of Kiesha, as I continued the writing. The conversations furthered as King Solomon planned for Kiesha to meet with him to drive him out of town. Finally, he gave us the address, and I called the Decatur Police Department. I informed them of what was about to occur and advised them to join us or receive a call afterwards. I drove my mother in law's van to the location where King Solomon waited for Kiesha, as unmarked police cars waited. We waited and waited. As Tonya sat angrily in the passenger's seat, she told me I had lost my mind. I gave up and we drove home. That evening the phone rang. A police car waited overnight near the house, and when King Solomon finally left, he was followed and arrested.

To my family, the media, and everyone across town I was deemed almost a superhero. I didn't care about that. I just wanted to give my family peace. I assured Tonya that it was safe for her to come home, she refused.

"What else do I have to do? I'm busting my ass trying to be good enough for you! I just risked my entire life trying to give you just a peace of mind. Why am I even in this with you? I would have been better off had one of them shot me! I have been rejected by you over and over. Every time I turn around it's another man. Maybe I should have shot myself."

"I don't care what you do," she said carrying more clothes and my baby from the house. I closed the door behind her. The house was empty, quiet, and cold. It was not a home. Chelsey and Alaura were with Tonya and Nicholas was in Mississippi with his mother. I had no friends. I had nothing. I walked to the dining room table that also served as my desk. I sat, dried my eyes, and dialed.

"Hello?" a voice said softly. "Well, this is a surprise."

"Hello. Hey Nikki."

# CHAPTER SEVEN

## WHAT LIES BENEATH

Too often, we enter into relationships, opportunities, and situations that require us to have healed, having experienced absolutely no healing whatsoever. I believe that whenever opportunities to heal present themselves to you, all the dark places of your past will attempt to resurface for one last stand. Once you leave the toxic relationships in your life, embrace the pain, and even find something to do in your downtime, you have to be prepared for the potential to relapse.

You must identify your internal and external triggers. Your internal triggers are in inner feelings, thoughts, and ideas that plague you with such suffering that they motivate you to return to the places you deemed harmful. Your exterior triggers are the literal people, places, or things that trigger you to go back into the toxic environments. Truthfully, you might be shocked to learn of some of the things you've always deemed as healthy may actually serve as triggers to the toxic places you've vacated. You have to exit those triggers as well.

At that moment, I realized rejection of my masculinity was my trigger. It had been so since I was raped as a boy. I had spent my entire life fighting to regain what was taken from me, and while all the world hailed me damn near Superman, to my wife and her family, I was still absolutely nothing. I could not handle that feeling on that day in question. So, that feeling triggered me, and it triggered to relapse to Nikki, the only one who ever made me feel my masculinity wasn't broken.

"It's been eleven years since I heard your voice," she said.

"I wasn't sure if you still had the same number."

"I hear you married Tonya. I always told you she wanted you," she laughed.

"She didn't want me. She just wanted you to think she wanted me," I said. "Are you married?"

"Yes, I'm married. We're separated now, and he's taken the kids."

"Oh, damn. I'm sorry." I was surprised of how forthcoming she was so suddenly, but this was Nikki.

"It's a long story. It's so good to hear your voice. My first love. My one true love," she said. I exhaled. Tonya had not told me she loved me in two years, and we regularly argued over it.

"Look, is it okay if I call you or text sometime. I don't know why. I just need to."

"Of course. Call me whenever. I'll be happy to talk with you. Nobody will ever know either one of us like the other," she said. I said goodbye and hung up the phone. I felt horribly guilty, as if I had cheated on Tonya. Then I became angry at Tonya. I wondered how it was so easy for her to entertain so many other men while it was killing me to have one phone call with Nikki.

Things could not have been worse with Tonya. The end of the year neared, and I had not spoken to Nikki again. Soon after that, I was informed by Tonya's cousin Tiffany that a relationship with Tonya and Tiffany's husband had been brought to the family's attention. I had overheard phone calls in which Tonya exposed to her family that Tiffany's husband had made attempts to sleep with her. I considered Tiffany's husband a friend. He was a fellow minister, and I often supported his ministry efforts. When I called to confront him, Tiffany detailed a very different truth to me. I listened quietly as she told me a different story and concluded with saying that she knew that Tonya was her cousin, and she knew the real Tonya. I believed her.

In my anger, I became attracted to Tiffany. I wanted her deeply, not because I could see a future with her, but because we were both married to the same toxic people. As she told me of our spouses, I could hear in her voice what I felt in my soul. I knew that like me, it was only her love of and fear of disappointing God that was keeping her in her marriage. She was humiliated. She was ragged from the tales of her husband and other women. Her story was my story. The more embarrassment I felt, the more I craved her. In my dreams, and in my mind, I wanted her. For months I could not close my eyes without thinking of Tiffany. But I knew, I did not truly want her. I wanted to hurt Tonya in retaliation. I could not, and I would not present my lust to Tiffany. I refused to have my character and reputation stained with an act so heinous. Both couples would move on as family as if nothing occurred.

I forced myself to ignore the latest revelation. I wanted a new start on my marriage. So, I bought flowers, cider, and candles. I wanted Tonya and me to renew our wedding vowels as the new year arrived with our children present. She declined, as her family desired to all go to church together. By this time, I began to hate her church outings with her family because they all resulted in me learning of a new man in my wife's life. She refused to renew our vowels and she left for her mother's house. I went to bed alone. Fifteen minutes before the clock struck twelve, I heard the kitchen door open. She entered the house and made her way to the bedroom. She turned on the lights.

"Get up. Let's renew our vowels," she said.
"What are you doing? I thought you were supposed to be at church?"
"Everybody decided they were too tired to go to church tonight," she explained.

"So, you're here to renew your wedding vowels because your family was too tired to go to church? Go to hell, Tonya."

"Don't say I didn't try," she said, walking into the bathroom. I heard the shower begin. Angry, I threw the covers off of me and made my way to the kitchen table to write. I needed to release. I logged on to Facebook to see all the happy people celebrating the New Year. A message appeared from Nikki wishing me a Happy New Year. The next message was followed by photos of her having sex with herself. She sent images after images of her inserting objects into her body; I was not aroused. Instead, I was saddened and shocked. I listened to be sure the shower was still running, and I stepped into the cold garage with my cell phone.

"Happy New Year. You get my pictures?"
"Yea. Happy New Year."

"What do you think? You know Birmingham isn't that far from you?" I didn't respond. "Tell me what you think?"

"I am thinking how the hell are you still the same person after all these years? How are you still this?"

"Who were you wanting me to be? That is the problem! You always wanted me to be someone else, and that's the reason you're not happy with Tonya either. You want her to be someone else too!"

"I hate you. I don't even know why I bothered with you." I hung up the phone. I looked at the sky to see fireworks. Minutes later, I felt my phone vibrating.

"What?", I said to Nikki.

"I'm sorry. You're right. I'm sorry. I'm really messed up," she cried.

"No, I'm sorry. I just don't know what I'm doing anymore."

"You were right. I am a horrible person. I tried to shoot him. I've done some bad things to all the men I loved."

"You tried to shoot who?"

"My husband. I went to jail. I'm probably going back to jail. I should have been in jail a long time ago. You should have sent me to jail. Maybe I would have gotten some type of help and been released by now, a better woman." There was a silence.

"Nikki, why would I have sent you to jail?", I said calmly. "Nikki, stop crying and answer me."

"No matter what, I loved you. I love you just as much today as I loved you then."

"Nikki, I loved you with everything in me, but I need you to tell me the truth. It's been eleven years. I don't care anymore. I just need the truth.", I pleaded.

"I just need your forgiveness. I'm so sorry. I have lived in torture since I left Tuscumbia. I need you to forgive me."

"Nikki, I forgive you for the things I know and the things I do not know. I forgive you for not knowing how to heal, and I pray you can forgive me also. We both weren't given fair shots to start with. You can be better than this."

"Thank you, my love," she said before hanging up. Nikki was found dead in her bed the following week. I sat with Tonya and the kids in her mother's living room when my brother Dowand called with the news. Tonya stared at my face as he told me of her death. The details surrounding the cause of death were secret. I hung up the phone. Tonya waited on me to speak.

"Nikki is dead."

"How? What happened?"

"I don't know. They don't know. No one is saying. I need to call her mother."

"What? Why?", she asked standing.

"I don't know. I need to hear it from her. I need to offer my condolences. I need to see how Nikki's daughter is doing."

"Why?", she shouted.

"Because my life didn't just start the day I met you!"

"Don't yell at me! Why are you looking like you are about to cry?", she retaliated as she held Alaura. I stared. "After everything she did to you, you're standing in front of me as if you are about to cry."

"I'm going to go get some drinks for the house." I grabbed the keys and exited the house. I sat in the seat of my car just in time for my heart to break. I wept. I cried.

I moved my son Nicholas into the house with us the next year. He absolutely thrilled me. The house seemed to be magical when he was there, but Tonya despised him. She resented his presence, but I knew that he needed me at this point in his life. He was a teen. He knew that she disliked him. She could not understand my need for him and his need for me. I needed to see that he was safe. Desperate to make her understand, I bared my lifelong truth to her. I told her that I was molested. I told her the identity of the molester. My greatest hurt would become her greatest weapon against me.

By this time, she had become violently destructive and bitter. She hated the idea of me being close to anyone. You see, Tonya's life was spent at her mother's house, where she would also take Chelsey and Alaura leaving me in our home alone. But when Nicholas came, I did not feel alone. I stopped arguing, and I became a different person. Prior to Nicholas moving in, my depression had led me to high blood pressure and more health complications as I weighed over 310lbs. As soon as my son arrived, I found more motivation to be healthier. Within a matter of months, I had shed 50lbs.

I was happier, and that happiness incited rage in her. Nicholas had wrestled with bone and muscle pains for quite a while. While he slept on the sofa often, many times I would urge him to take Alaura's bed. Alaura's bed was a twin-size bed, and she slept nights in my arms. While I would still permit him to sleep in Alaura's bed, those nights would lead to heated angry attacks in our bedroom as Tonya threatened to burn Alaura's bed whenever Nicholas slept in it.

The life I hated as a child I now lived. The woman I loved more than God no longer existed. The wife I knew was no more. She hated the sight of me. I would wrestle her to the ground to avoid her attempt to throw a hot pan of grease in my face. Threats to kill me, herself, and the children were now a norm. I feared allowing her to drive us after she made several attempts to crash the family into a ditch with us all inside. I feared being like my father so much, that I could not even stand up against a woman. I had spent so many years pretending that our marriage was perfect, that I knew no one would believe me if I ever exposed the truth. My greatest performance was regarding my happy home. I had been taught to do this by my parents. We helped share the tales that it was a shoebox that fell from my mother's closet shelf that led to her bruised eye.

By now, the sequel to *Diamonds* opened, and matters were even worse. In an effort to include her more in the operations of the company, I allowed her to assist in booking cities for the next tour. I felt wonderful. I had built a production company and I was now able to pay my cast, crew, and production team. Tonya began working on the Nashville performance. She invited a Nashville pastor named Roger aboard to assist. She and her family were accustomed to visiting and singing at his church, so she convinced me he would be a great voice in the area to help promote the tour.

As the plans continued, I found text messages in her phone of her asking Roger if he would consider having an affair with her. To my humiliated relief, he turned her down. I was so furious and humiliated for another man to tell my wife to go home and take her vows seriously. I raged at the fact that she would allow me to bring my entire company to Nashville to work with a man she desired to have an affair with. I called off the Nashville show and aimed to keep the matter secret.

Everything began to crumble. It never dawned on me that Roger shared the same last name as one of my actresses, also from Nashville. So, the whispers began. I forwarded the text messages to Tonya's family out of anger, and she retaliated with more threats. We neared another new year and perhaps the next new year could be different. Instead, Tonya informed me that she was going to church with her family again, and they were going to Roger's church. I was furious at the audacity that she would even go to his church knowing what had occurred, but she insisted.

I felt the end was nearing, so I began secretly videoing and recording the threats and heinous acts in the house. She found joy in assuring me that no one would ever believe me over her. She told me that no doctor or judge would ever see that side of her; perhaps she was right. I began wondering what my life would have been like had I not married Tonya.

I began receiving requests to write for much larger companies. The tours were over, so I opted to create a dramatic series. I grew tired of waiting for someone to put me on television, so I decided to put myself on television. I would write, film, and produce the series and air the drama online and in late-night paid programming cable TV spots I purchased across the south. It was a new venture. I loved live audiences, but this method would put my content in homes all across the south weekly, and my sponsors would cover the cost and leave me with a great profit. So, I began writing the new series. I would walk door – to - door of local startups aiming to sell thirty or sixty second commercials to the companies.

Again, sinking in suspicion, I logged into Tonya's phone again to find the most recent messages to men. I was crushed. Romantic messages were communicated with a young man I viewed as family. I was very close to his family. So close, that I respected his mother as a sister. So, I did not call to confront BJ. Instead, I called to speak to his mother to let her know I was about to confront him.

"I just found messages in my wife's phone to another man she has something going on with," I said into the phone.

"You must be talking about my son," she said casually.

"You know?"

"He told me the night it started. We all know. I told him not to go there, but he is a grown man. I know how he is with older women."

I did not know what else to do. I called the aunt Tonya respected the most, I called Esther. She was the one I respected the most. She and her husband had survived troublesome times in the past, and they seemed to be a joined unit. If ever there was anyone who could say something to help save our marriage, it would be her. I had gone to so many other preachers and pastors for help. Everything failed. I pleaded with Esther to help. I showed her the messages Tonya sent to the men. I showed her the messages, and threats to kill herself and everyone in the home. I bared my soul to her as I sat on the phone in an empty parking lot. She told me just to hang tight. She would pray, and God would show her how to help. I felt relieved.

It was one week later when I saw a flier on social media advertising Esther's women's empowerment conference. The flier showed Esther with her arms stretched wide in the header and details of a stage play Tonya had written that featured BJ on the flier as well. I was furious. I had shared my soul pleading for Esther to help save our marriage, and instead, she was preparing to put Tonya and BJ in the pulpit together before her congregation to minister. I was angry. I was humiliated. Everything was changing. I was changing. I walked onto the deck of my house as I tried to gather myself. I was tired in a way that a man should never grow tired. Tonya was on a warpath to destroy me and there was no denying it any longer. It was the truth. It was my truth, and her hatred towards me was increasing with every passing day.

I believe it is important in life to always question yourself. Don't always blame yourself, but always question yourself. I questioned my role in her mental and emotional state. A short while later, I encountered the Prophetess Gloria in a grocery store. I had not spoken to her in many years. Her dress was dirty and torn. She carried a switch with her that she had just used on the legs of a young boy she pulled alongside of her. When I informed her of our marriage and the painful experience it had been the entire time, she told me that I was never supposed to take her prophecy seriously. It wasn't meant to be taken literally, she explained before casually walking away. I followed behind her to tell her that she made me believe that God would punish me if I disobeyed and refused to marry Tonya. She told me that I misunderstood and offered prayer. I declined. I walked out of the store.

As a kid, my favorite drink was a chocolate Yoo-Hoo. Whenever I could convince my mother to let me accompany her to the grocery store, I would plead with her to buy me the drink. I didn't want the drink in the can; I wanted the drink in the glass bottle. As soon as we would make it back to the car, I knew that I had only a few moments to consume the drink before we made it back home and my Mom would be forced to explain why she bought me something from the store and not my brothers. So, I would hurry and down the drink in one gulp it seemed.

Upon finishing the drink, I would lower the cold beverage from my lips and recap it. Then I would notice the brown residue still in the bottom of the glass. Next, I would always read the words on the side of the bottle, urging drinkers to shake the bottle before drinking for the best taste. I would see these words every time I drank the chocolate drink, but because I was in such a rush to drink it, I never took the time to shake it. Eventually, I was determined that I would actually slow myself and follow the suggested directions so I could taste the drink at its best, and I did so.

To my surprise, I hated the new taste. I had spent so many years drinking the lesser version of the drink, that by the time I actually had the drink in the manner in which it was created, I did not like it. This is exactly what I would come to discover about my life as I came to understand my role in the demise of my marriage, and all the relationships I had during that time. There was something happening in every relationship I had with the people in my life, and I could not deny it. I obtained friends, family, and even a wife before I took time to allow God to heal me, shake me, and bring the best of me to the surface. I presented myself as already healed. I performed as a healed man. I ran companies as a healed man. I preached as a healed man, and I wrote as a healed man. So, everyone in my life who loved me, loved the me I gave them to love. But, somewhere along the line I desired to be better, and in the flicker of a moment, God began shaking me together in a way I had never been together before. All those around me who loved the version of me they were accustomed to, could not digest who I was now becoming. Was it their fault? Was it my fault? Was it anyone's fault?

This realization took my breath away. Tonya had not changed. I had changed, and she had no taste for who I was becoming as I healed. My healing was suffocating the life out of her. She had shown me since the beginning that she was not in love with me, but I still led her into the dark trails that became our lives as I continued running from my childhood. I realized at that moment that I had led Tonya into a marriage as a prescription to an illness she was never qualified to heal.

She adored her family. She wanted to be at her mother's house everyday laughing, celebrating, and enjoying her family. I no longer resented that. For seven years I begged her to make our home her home; our home was not her home. If she found her joy, peace, and healing in the arms of her family, why would I pull her from that? And just like that, I forgave Tonya. Not because she ever apologized, but because I put her in a game she showed me she could not win. I did not care. I just needed to be in the game. In that moment, all the indiscretions and hurt was not solely upon her, and I owned that. I remembered Nikki telling me following the end of our relationship, that no woman would ever be good enough for me. You know what? I now know that she was right. She was right because I was not falling in love for love. I was falling in love for a new life, and whenever the relationship went in a direction contrary to what made me feel safe, I would lose myself. Nikki was dead, but I could offer some sort of apology to Adrianna and Tonya. I needed Adrianna's forgiveness. I knew that I broke her heart. I sent her messages and emails acknowledging the state I was in during our relationship. It was my prayer that she never blamed herself or felt that she was not enough. I wanted to clean up so much that my pain had broken. I waited for Adrianna to respond.

So, further walking in the first steps of my truth and my peace, I told Tonya I wanted a divorce. She was silent. I assured her that I would stay for six months, so it is not a sudden break for the family. I walked out of the kitchen, and I knew that it was right. It felt right. I just had to make it six months. She seemed to not believe me. For a while, she became the perfect spouse. We even had sex again, for the first time in over a year. But it could not fix us. I felt relieved that the sex did not fix us.

I no longer wanted to stay. I informed the cast of why I cried in between takes, and they covered me in every way that I needed to be covered. The show premiered on several CW cable networks. I tried to focus on work during the final months at home. Tonya began to cook. She began staying home. I wanted to let her know that she did not have to do those things. They were not needed. I wanted her to continue doing the things that fed her soul. She would need to be at her best for what was to come when the world would learn of our separation.

She began being nicer to Nicholas. That meant the world to me. It brightened my soul, but still, it would not fix us. You see, by this time I had peace with my pain. The pain was not okay, but the pain was mine to make okay. And by now, I was ready to work on the pain. As the road to the separation date continued, her behavior worsened. The children shared with me their concerns over her mental state. It would be during dinner when I heard Tonya make a sexual remark to Nicholas. I froze. I had spent my entire childhood waiting for someone to stand up for me against sexual innuendos and gestures. I refused to allow my son to be subjected to it in my house.

"What the hell did you just say to him?", I shouted.

"It was a joke. He knows I was joking," she laughed.

"It was a sexual joke. You told him that you didn't think he could grind in you like I do!"

"I was just joking!"

"That is my son! My sixteen-year-old son! He's supposed to be like your son! I couldn't even think of making a sexual comment towards Chelsey! You are out of your fucking mind."

"No, you're out of your fucking mind! Just because you got raped and molested doesn't mean somebody is trying to do the same thing to him. I should call Jeff right now and let him know that you're saying he molested you." She held her phone as she stood in the bathroom, raging at me. I shook my head and walked away.

I had to figure out a plan of exit. Tonya was not mentally stable, and I feared leaving suddenly with Nicholas. I feared what might happen to the other children. I knew I was nearing the end of the six months, but I could not leave Nicholas there anther minute. The next day I returned him to his mother's home. I would not see my son again for another year. I believed he felt I chose Tonya over him, so he avoided me. Instead, I believed he had another place safe to go. I had nowhere else for the other children, so I felt I had to stay there with them. Maybe I was right, maybe I was wrong, but I was trying to make difficult decisions for everyone, including Tonya. You see, our home was extremely toxic by this time. Could she actually follow through on her threats to hurt herself, the children, or me? I don't know. I didn't know, but I did know that I grew up in the same home. I could not allow my children to witness what I witnessed. I feared she was nearing a psychotic break.

When it comes to marriage, you never truly know a person until you have had time to observe who they are in various seasons of life. You need to know who they are when they're with money, without money, or when you are with or without money. You need to know who they are when they are sad, jealous, tempted, grieving and when they don't get their way. People don't change after marriage, seasons change. If you've married them and you haven't witnessed who your spouse is beyond the easy-going season, then you are in for the shock of your life.

A few days later, I dropped off Tonya and the other kids at her mother's home. They were going to church. Twenty minutes would pass before Tonya called crying instructing me to meet her at a gas station to pick them up. Feeling something was wrong, I hurried to the small store. When I arrived, Tonya loaded the children in the car as they all cried. An argument had occurred among the family, and Tonya had attempted to jump from the moving van. I was shocked. The children were terrified, and I did not know what to do. Before we made it out of the parking lot, Tonya changed her mind and decided she still wanted to go to church with her family.

A few hours later, I watched the live video on social media of her singing at the church they visited as if nothing had occurred. I closed the phone. My head hurt, and I felt as if I was trying to control a hurricane inside of me. The phone rang. I refused to answer. The phone rang again. Eventually, I lifted the phone to my ear and spoke.

"Hello?" I said to a friend.

"Yella Box, you sitting down?"

"Why? What's wrong?", I asked truly not caring as I did not care regarding many things during that time. He ignored my tone, and replied

"Man, it's Adrianna. She's dead."

# CHAPTER EIGHT

## THE CUSSING

"I'm going also.", Tonya said. By the time she had arrived home that night, she had already learned of Adrianna's death. She immediately came to me. I informed her that I would attend Adrianna's funeral. I can still remember the feeling of the breath leaving my body at that moment when I was told Adrianna had died. She had lost a long battle with Lupus, and her beautiful spirit left our world. "I'm going to the funeral also." She repeated.

"Tonya, don't be disrespectful. You did not like her at all, and her friends knew it. Do not be disrespectful!"

"If you're going, I'm going."

"Why? We are divorcing. We are separating in a few weeks. I'm sick of you trying to make everyone think that everything is fine with us. Things are not fine. I know what you are doing. Once I leave, and I am leaving, you will pretend as if you were clueless to everything."

"I'm going to the funeral.", she said, walking from the bedroom. I deeply needed closure, but I refused to enter Adrianna's funeral with Tonya. So I did not attend the service. I had begun informing people around me that I would be moving out in the coming weeks. I already had an apartment, which was such a milestone. I felt liberated just by signing the lease.

However, Tonya was doing the direct opposite. She was further illustrating to the world a false depiction that everything was perfect. She was misleading family and friends into believing we were planning a romantic getaway for our upcoming wedding anniversary. She dismissed all rumors of a pending divorce. I was asked to become a worship leader at a church in my hometown. I told Pastor Brian that I would assist for a few months, but I did not feel it was appropriate for me to be in such a role once my separation would occur. The Pastor assured me that it was fine for me to serve in such a role following a divorce, that even he had been married three times and never stopped preaching from the pulpit every Sunday. I believed him.

I continued in the position of worship leader as well. I had no idea that running a company while preparing for such a difficult time would take such a toll on me, so I began to fumble with *Kats*. The cast and crew worked to keep me motivated and to keep pushing, but I was running out of ambition, focus, drive, and peace. Before long, I could not prepare myself for the divorce and produce the television show at the same time. I pulled the show from cable television. I felt as if I failed, but I needed to focus on the children and be certain they were prepared. My income diminished significantly as I relied on my salary from the church. The plan was for all bills to be covered and covered in advance upon me moving out. I did not want to leave Tonya in financial ruins. That part of the plan was perfectly intact. I would now start my new life with nothing, but I was ready.

It felt amazing to me to be amongst a new church where there was no Malone insight, but Tonya forced her way into the car to join me every Sunday. We argued. I did not want the new faces becoming accustomed to her face as Tonya and I both knew we would separate in a matter of months, but she insisted on attending. Following moments in which I would sing, I would sit in the choir loft, dry the tears and sweat from my face. I would pull my vibrating phone to me. She would text me vulgarity and attacks on my voice during the service. I struggled to perform with her present. Finally, enough was enough.

.        "Tonya, we need to work out some of these final details," I said, entering the bedroom.

"You ain't going nowhere," she said.

"Tonya, stop tripping. Now you're keeping the house, all the furniture in the house, and you're buying a new car this week. I'll just take the old car. This doesn't have to get ugly. It's no reason for it to get ugly. If we act a fool, our families will act a fool."

"Trust me; it's going to get ugly. You haven't seen ugly yet."

"Why? Why does it have to get ugly? You stepped out of our marriage from the day of the wedding until this day? You admitted that you didn't love me. We've had sex ten times in seven years. Why do you have to act ugly now that I'm leaving?"

"I never had sex with any of those men!"

"I don't give a damn if you did or not. It wouldn't have hurt any less. Now I'm going, and it's not going to get ugly. You're going to act like you have some fucking sense! I am not a mat you can just walk over!", I shouted.

"Please. Nobody likes you. Nobody ever believes you. Nikki made sure of that," She laughed.

"Fuck you and Nikki too. One thing I learned from Nikki is to never allow an evil woman to have power over me again. They'll believe this." I played an audio recording on my phone. Her eyes bulged as she listened to the screams and sounds of the car nearly crashing in a ditch as she threatened to kill us all because she was unable to attend a church service with her family. "That's just the beginning. I have every screenshot, every recording, and every message of everything you did to torture me the last year." She stared. "Tonya, I have no intentions of anyone ever seeing or hearing any of this, as long as you let me go in peace. That's it. I don't want to fight, and I don't want the kids hurt. I just want to go. I won't raise them in this. I walked away leaving her speechless on the bed.

I carried Alaura into the backyard. I sat on the deck as I watched Alaura race to the slide in her playhouse. She was so precious and had no idea of the home she lived in. I exhaled. Tonya stepped onto the deck.

"Give me the phone," she said.

"Tonya, I'm not giving you this phone."

"Fine. I'll just go straight to the cell phone company and have them turn the phone off. You won't be able to send anything to anyone and all your tv friends, sponsors, and celebrities won't have a phone number to call you on. So, you have nothing to use against me," she stated. She knew how important that particular phone number was to me. To change phone numbers at that time could unbelievably damage my career.

"You don't think I anticipated how evil you are? Go to the phone company. I already had the number switched over to another carrier months ago. I knew you would try that."

She pulled a knife from behind her back.

"I said give me the phone."

"Tonya, are you crazy? Really?" She waved the knife at me.

"You're not going to show that to anyone." I jumped from the chair. With her eyes wet and dark, she lunged at me. I kicked the chair towards her missing the knife as I jumped from the deck.

"Daddy!" Alaura's tiny voice echoed as Tonya raced after me with the knife above her head. Even as I ran from her, I feared she would trip and fall on the knife herself. I stopped running. I turned to her. I informed her of the neighbors who gardened in their backyard next door.

"This ain't over. I ain't done. I'll slit your fucking throat!", she said, shaking her head. She pulled Alaura into her arms. I reached for my daughter. Tonya, raged and raced to her car and sped away. Out of breath, I called my aunt. I struggled for breath as I informed her what had occurred. She was out of town, so she made calls herself. Within a matter of moments, the doorbell rang. It was Tonya's family.

I attempted to explain with not much luck the truth behind our marriage. No one believed me. I played the recordings. I informed them that Tonya had known for the recent six months that I was moving out. I informed them of my concern over her mental state. When her mother asked me why I had not informed them earlier, I stated that I had pleaded with Esther for help months prior. They waited in the living room and attempted to call Tonya. She avoided us all. Eventually, they left in search of her. I loaded my final belongings into my car, and I left the home.

I opened the door to my new apartment. I did not know what to think. I sat on the sofa. Within moments the world began to call. My parents, my siblings, and my friends all informed me of the mistake I was making and that I would destroy the children, my marriage, my ministry, and my career. It was not a deal-breaker to my parents or my siblings for my wife to swing a butcher's knife at my throat. They all urged me to work on the marriage and informed me of rough patches in their own relationships.

My niece, however, was not raised in the home with us under my parents. So, our norm, was not her norm. I was only eight when Shonte was born. She had always been more of a sister to me than a niece. I do not condone violence, but Shonte gave me peace, love, and strength by the rage she exampled as a result of Tonya's behavior. Tonya called me terrified and demanding I call off Shonte. I convinced Shonte to not engage in physical altercations, but she responded in a way to validate where I had healed. This type of love was not love. It was not healthy, and more than I needed air- I needed someone who loved me to say such treatment was wrong. None of the Christian figures in my life told me it was wrong. Many told me to just pray or find a woman on the side.

I prayed and thanked God for enabling me to never return violence towards Tonya. I could have never hit her. Never. Had I hit her, I certainly would have killed myself. I could not have lived with myself. In anger, I once told her that there was something wrong with her brain. The look on her face at that moment is still burned into my mind today. I apologized to her for those words repeatedly.

While sitting on my new sofa in my new home, I called Pastor Brian for prayer. Little did I know that he had been making attempts to sleep with Tonya. I realized that I would need assistance getting my last large items up the stairs into my home. So, that night Kendrick showed up to assist with unloading my car. I felt dead, absolutely dead. I did not talk much as we carried my television upstairs. As we made our way back to the vehicle, I saw Tonya driving her mother's van.

"I told you it wasn't over," she said. I looked into the backseat to see Alaura.

"How did you find me?"

"Hey, Tonya," Kendrick said. She did not address him. He had worked for us for many years and was like family.

"I called the utility department and pretended to be you. I asked them for the other address on the account. You see, I'm smarter than you," she said.

"Hey Daddy," Alaura smiled.

"Hey, Baby. Tonya, you need to leave," I said. She looked around me to see Kendrick unloading items from my car.

"I guess you fucking him, huh?", Tonya said.

"How can you say some shit like that in front of her?"

"You let Jeff mess with you!"

"Are you serious? I was five! You need help, Tonya!"

"You brought Kendrick into our house and let him sleep downstairs. You know he acts like a fag! I bet he is why you are leaving."

"Are you serious? You offered to let him sleep on our couch a few days because he was homeless and sleeping in a park during a snowstorm! I just agreed to what YOU suggested!"

"I was testing you! Any decent man would have said, NO!", she snapped

"You need to leave before I have you arrested," I replied.

"Lori, look at Daddy and his boyfriend," she stated. I walked away. I made my way to my car. I drove away as she followed behind me, attempting to hit my car. I dialed one of Tonya's aunts.

"Look, I'm doing everything I can to not hit her, fight her, or have her arrested. Can somebody please do something?" I hung up the phone. A few moments later Tonya drove away. I made my way back to my apartment. Kendrick stood next to his car in shock. I instructed him to leave. I turned my phone off as Tonya texted that she would make every person in the world hate me, including Alaura. The apartment was dark, cold, and empty. It was only me.

The next morning, the battle furthered. Everyone and everything connected to me was under attack. Rumors spread that Tonya had caught me and another man having sex, and she ended the marriage. Pastor Brian soon after called a meeting with the church deacons to inform them that they needed to get rid of me because he believed Tonya's accusations. He knew that I learned of his pursuit of Tonya, so he feared I would expose him. I was accused of having sex with every man and woman that were close friends. I called my Grandmother. In all her beauty, she gave me strength again.

"Baby, when people are afraid you will tell the truth about them, they will tell a lie on you. When folks can't deny the truth, they'll attack the person telling the truth. Focus on God," she said. She knew this day would come. She did not push for it or push me towards it. She waited on my exit in the most organic way possible. She waited until I grew my way out. I told her that I loved her.

I remembered a box I had forgotten at the house. Certain Tonya was not there I returned to retrieve the box. Upon arriving at the home, I was met by Child Protective Services. A neighbor had witnessed the incident in the backyard and reported the incident to the authorities. I wanted Tonya to receive help, and I knew that she was capable of killing herself if I was not gentle with her. It had been quite some time since I had retired from social work, but I pleaded with former colleagues and friends to make this matter disappear. I called Tonya to inform her of what was occurring. She seemed frightened, but still denied the occurrence with the knife. It was almost as if she could not remember the incident. Alaura, being only 4 spoke of her mother chasing her father with a knife. Tonya, still denied the incident, until Alaura eventually stopped speaking of it.

I felt a sense of responsibility to the children as well as Tonya. I sat on the brink of insanity, fearing that any moment Child Protective Services would arrive to remove the children from Tonya. I knew that she would not survive. My former boss called me and told me the matter was erased. She was facing charges for fraud and assured me that if I would not testify in court against her that she would see to it that the investigation against Tonya went away. I agreed. I called Tonya to tell her the matter was erased. She did not seem to care. She was furious because I had cussed so many of her family members who worked to spread the untruths.

I sat in the driveway of what was once our home for the last time. I knew that Tonya would never return to get clothes, furniture, or much of anything from the house. The house was never her home. There was always enough of her belongings at her mother's home. The phone rang again. I did not feel like arguing or fighting any further, and I did not feel like explaining my decision to anyone. However, I did answer.

"Hello?"

"Man, you fucking up! What you doing?", a voice said. I immediately became angry. I knew the voice. The voice was familiar, and the voice was family. The voice was Jeff.

"Don't call my fucking phone like that! Who do you think you're talking to?", I shouted. He was silent for a moment. He had never heard me speak in such a way, neither had I. He spoke.

"Man, I'm just trying to help. I don't want to see you messing up your life. Now, Tonya is a good woman. You need to give up this Hollywood dream. You ain't gonna be no writer. You need to focus on Tonya. I'm telling you what I know."

"You don't know shit about me or Tonya, or anything going on in my life or my family!"

"I know that she saying she caught you in bed with a man! You need to stop posting selfies of you now that you've lost weight. Folks already think light-skinned men are gay and you out here posting pictures of yourself looking gay!" He said.

"Let me explain something to you." I began as my chest tightened. "Three hundred and ten pounds I weighed when I was in my miserable marriage to Tonya. I wanted to kill myself every day. To a fucked-up person like you, being depressed, fat, and broken is masculine! Now that I have the confidence to take a selfie of myself happy and healthy, you want to attack my sexuality? You know what? Fuck you and everyone else who has a problem with anything I do. You molested me most of my childhood, and you have the nerve to call me and attack my marriage and manhood. Fuck you. Don't call me again!", I raged.

My heart raced. I wasn't' sure when I had begun driving, but I was speeding down the interstate. Seconds later, Jeff texted informing me that he's never done anything but tried to help me. He further texted that he did not know what I was talking about.

I felt like screaming. I felt as if the entire world had gone mad. I did not expect or need him to confirm what he had done to me. Any innocent person wrongfully accused of such, certainly would have done much more than send a simple text message as if he was a victim. I knew I was nearing another panic attack, so I made an exit, and I parked.

"What did you say?", the voice said from the car. Unable to remember when I had dialed or began conversing, I recognized my mother's voice sounding through my car's speaker system. I gasped for air. "He said he was molested." I heard her repeat to my father.

"Mama, from age five to nine I was molested. Jeff molested me." I freed myself.

"What?", she shouted. "He just said Jeff molested him when he was a little boy." She repeated to my father. I could not hear my father's words, but his murmurs. She spoke again. "That's a lie. I don't believe that for a second."

"Call him and ask him! I already confronted him about it, and if he was innocent, he would have called you both and told you that I had accused him of such a lie. If he hasn't called you, that's the proof! Why would I lie about this?"

"I don't believe you for one second! I don't believe you. You're just trying to tear down somebody else because your life is torn down," she shouted into my soul.

# CHAPTER NINE

## THE ART OF THE EXIT

### *Summer 2019*

Sometimes the ceiling fan appears to spin in the opposite direction if you stare at it long enough. This was my realization as I still rested beneath my large white bed comforter. I exhaled and glanced at my phone for the time. It was 9:00 AM, and if I was going to make the drive to Muscle Shoals in time, I would have to leave soon. I did not want to make the drive. I did not want to pull myself from the bed, but my feet eventually hit the floor.

I stood and headed for the main bathroom. I did not use the master bathroom because the scale is kept in the main bathroom. It had become a pattern to weigh myself on Sunday mornings. I passed Alaura's bedroom. I paused and looked inside. The bedroom was empty, but beautiful. I smiled, thinking of her visits and the smile on her face when we make homemade slime in her bedroom. I continued down the hallway past the next bedroom. I glanced inside, and for a moment, I could see Nicholas sitting on the bed and Chelsey at the computer desk. I then entered the bathroom and stepped onto the scale. I stared at the 185lb reading. I knew then that I would get dressed and make the drive. So, I dressed and walked down the stairs into the empty great room. I grabbed my keys from the piano and headed out the door. I drove to a nearby gas station where I realized the car had a flat tire. Then I quickly noticed a hole in the tire and knew the car could not make it to Muscle Shoals.

I felt relieved and almost happy. I returned home and shut off the engine. I sat in the car and pulled my phone from my pocket. I would text my mother to inform her that I could not attend my father's sermon due to a bad tire. I began to text when I realized I owned another vehicle sitting in my driveway. The complete financial, physical, and emotional turnaround of my life stared me in the face. So, I returned the phone to my pocket, switched vehicles, and headed to Muscle Shoals.

Almost two hours later, I arrived at the small church. I recognized the vehicles of my siblings. I recognized my parent's car. I turned off the engine and sat in the car for a few moments. My nephew made his way from the church to his parents' car near me. I rolled down my car window.

"Hey, man."

"Hey, Yella Box,." he smiled. I smiled also.

"Has your Granddaddy started preaching yet?"

"No, not yet. I think he's next though," he explained before returning to the church. I exited the car and headed for the church as well. I had not seen my parents in over a year. I had not visited their home, and I had rarely accepted phone calls. I made my way into the sanctuary. I sat in the rear as I identified my family. There was no music, and the pastor sang. I was still in awe that my father could be in any place where he was not in absolute control. A few moments later, my father's cane hit the floor and he pivoted himself onto his feet. He limped across the pulpit to the podium. He spoke slowly. He was much thinner than the last time I had seen him.

Just as I had watched him do my entire childhood, he requested my mother come to the front to sing before he preached. She turned to the rear to look for me, then motioned for me to play the organ. I did not want to budge as the organ appeared old, and I wasn't even sure if it worked, but I accompanied my mother. He continued standing as she stood behind him in the choir loft. Both of them, frail, brittle, and weak, wept as she sang *Precious Lord, Take my Hand*. His shouts of praise echoed throughout the sanctuary as her trembling hands stretched out to God. Her voice trembled and was weaker than I had ever known, but she gave it her all. While they were not touching, it was evident that they were helping one another to stand. At that moment, I knew they were tired. They were the kind of tired that I had never seen on them before. They had mentally and spiritually began preparing themselves for the final chapter of their lives.

The song ended, and she stumbled to return to her seat. I returned to my seat in the rear of the sanctuary. I felt hollow for a moment. A year had gone by since I had figured out the strategy for leaving my toxic relationship with my parents, and in that year, they seemed to have become more broken by life, sickness, and distress. But then, he spoke. And when he spoke, he spoke words we had never heard him say. To me, he cussed, and I loved it.

"I am truly grateful for my wife and for all of my children for being here this morning. It has been a long time since I stood to preach, and I thank you for being here. If I've never told you all this before, I love you all," and then he cried.

In 2013, a few weeks after telling my parents that Jeff molested me, my mother called me to apologize for her words. I do not know if her words meant she believed me, or if she was merely just sorry for her words. I did not know if she confronted Jeff. It did not matter to me. I forgave her. Sexual molestation in the black community is still the secret not shared. To be frank, most of the people chronicled in my story were all victims of sexual molestation and assault, but I was one of the only ones to eventually confront the trauma. You have to understand that just a little over 155 years ago rape and molestation amongst and towards blacks was not discussed or reported because it was a legal for-profit business. Slave masters would rape their slaves and breed older male slaves with younger female slaves to produce humans for inventory. There was no need for blacks to talk of it or complain because it was legal. We have blacks living today who are children of slaves, so the secrecy is taught to remain secret unless someone addresses the pain of molestation.

While I would love to say that my relationship with my parents improved in 2013, it did not. My mother's health declined, and we all knew we only had so much time left with her. She was dying of renal failure. To say that my mother was dying was to say that my father was dying also. But out of the shadows of her illness, came his love for her that we did not know existed.

We never witnessed our parents embrace, kiss, or tell the other they were loved. They withheld the same affection from us. It would be while she slept in a hospital bed, that for the first time I witnessed my father kiss her. I was in my mid 30's at the time. The fear in his eyes of losing her crippled him. They had spent almost fifty years together. By only a miracle, a family friend donated my mother a kidney. After she had spent her entire life catering and serving my father, he served her with gladness.

When did the toxicity end? To what capacity did it end? I do not know, and I do not want to give the impression that one should wait out the poison until it gets better. By no means should you do that, and by no means should my Mom have stayed. The means do not justify the end, because in the end leaves many scars on many people that I pray daily we can all heal from.

To remain in her marriage, my mother disconnected herself from everyone except my Dad.

A year prior to my father's significant sermon, I decided that I had to establish boundaries with my parents. I could not continue into my now successful career telling myself I am confident, capable, equipped, and blessed, only to have my interactions with my parents leave me in a pit of despair and brokenness for days. I clearly communicated a list of my Basic Primary Needs for them being in my life, and I refused to negotiate. Within a matter of months, after 35 years, I finally saw the changes I never thought were possible.

I will not take credit for whatever has transpired, but I had to do something for me. Setting boundaries is not pettiness. It is not revenge, and it is not retaliation. Setting boundaries is an act of love for one's self and for those they love. You must set boundaries with everyone in your life. Your parents, siblings, spouse, friends, boss, and children all need to know the boundaries they cannot dishonor and keep a seat in your life. You have to understand that my parents were never parents to us. They were our caretakers, and that is a big difference. So, whenever they were displeased with us, they disconnected from us as if we were no more than local town folk or friends. It would not trouble my parents to not see or speak to their children or grandchildren for months or even years. However, they had to have closeness with one another, no one else. As children, we never worried about food, shelter, money, or cars. However, my siblings and I all ran headfirst into the world looking for love, support, validation and loyalty.

Months before my father's sermon he surprised my siblings and I by inviting all his sons to breakfast. This had never happened before. Our entire lives we were almost taught to not have relationships with one another. My parents would have relationships with us individually, but they took measures to ensure their children would never be more loyal or bonded to one another than to them. So, when the family would gather for holidays, there was no closeness, and no one was happy but my parents. The rest of us felt we were in the company of strangers and almost enemies as our parents had led us to always believe about our siblings. I had healed in a way that I could see this, but some of my siblings still could not. By the time of my father's breakfast invitation, I was not ready to relax such a boundary with my parents. I refrained from going to the breakfast.

Families are notorious about avoiding conversation and not addressing the elephant in the room. I had grown weary of family dinners where no one connected, and everyone only tolerated one another. I had long since stopped putting myself in similar situations. An apology does not repair a relationship, but I stopped sharing time and space with people who cannot offer an acknowledgement of wrong. Failure to even acknowledge a mistake robs us of a hope of reconciliation. Since I had never seen my father apologize to anyone, I avoided the breakfast. I would no longer pressure anyone in my life to be anyone other than who they naturally were. Just as most other times, I was told by some family that I am being judgmental or harsh for my stern boundaries.

However, my boundaries are for me. Your boundaries are for you, and do not let anyone guilt you out of your boundaries. Usually, the people who will criticize you for maintaining your boundaries are people who have become comfortable with being bullied and treated poorly. You will be in your head alone fighting you alone. Following the breakfast, my siblings informed me that my father told them he never did anything of that sort of bonding with his own father. However, watching his children with their children inspired him to do more. This was a clear indication that I could relax a boundary. My father not only saw an error in his ways, but he had acknowledged his mistakes to those affected by his mistakes. That was monumental to me. If you do not give people the boundaries you expect from them, then you have nothing to grade them on as to how you should proceed with them.

There was a time in life in which I did not know that I had the authority to set boundaries with anyone, because my most precious boundary was crossed when I was a child. The truth is, that my innocence was not my boundary to establish. It was my parent's boundary to establish for me before the rest of the world, but they were so consumed with their own struggles that they did not set that boundary. They did not protect me, and you know what? I'm okay with that today. I am okay with the understanding that they were so ill prepared to be married, that they could not invest themselves into being the type of parents that were needed. My mother's goal was to learn to be the wife my father needed, and his goal was to train her to be the wife he needed. They never got around to being the type of parents their children needed. Instead, they gave us the parents that I believe were given to them.

And once I saw that, my parents became my children. The same patience, tolerance, and understanding I sought from them my entire life, I needed and wanted to give to them. My father was no longer a monster, he became a scared little boy who's fear of being alone devastated him. I just wanted to hold him. He greeted his children with a hug whenever we neared. Today remorse is permanently painted across his face, in his eyes, and in his presentation. I see it. His desire to grow and heal today is louder than any struggle I ever saw in him. He is affectionate, vulnerable, humble, kind, and supportive. It is my prayer that he can forgive himself as well. My mother became my rebellious teenage daughter. I had to give her space.

When I confronted Gloria in the grocery store, she informed me that if I actually knew God and His will for my life, then I would not have allowed anyone to convince me to marry the wrong woman - not even her. As angry as her words made me, she was right. She was more than right. I had spent my entire life in church. My Dad preached his first sermon 3 days after I was born. I had always known church, but God?

Who was God? My entire life He had been a weapon used for oppression, abuse, neglect, and manipulation. He was a weight on my back, and the god I was given was never a liberator. So, if God really existed, then I would have to find him outside of the church because I personally realized that organized religion was not conducive for my healing. I had witnessed murder, sex, lies, abuse, rape, adultery, and molestation by the most powerful people in organized religion, and the lack of accountability could not be of God.

The black church was founded during the years of American slavery, and still today no other race holds their spiritual leader to such regard as the black church. The leadership, governing, and discipline used by slave masters, became the same leadership used by many black pastors over their parishioners. It was the only leadership they knew. For many years the black church was not just the church to the black community, it was the city hall, civil rights headquarters, school, grocery store, and more. So, to disagree with the black pastor was equivalent to disagreeing with the President of The Black United States. The penalty of exile and facing God's wrath was dreadful.

So many years later, we still have black churchgoers who fear the wrath of their pastors. Toxic pastors control every aspect of the congregants' lives from their funds, relationships, and more. Some pastors sex their way through the congregations still just the same as the slave masters did. Now we have broken men and women who feel they have had no other value or significance anywhere else in the world, who then step into roles of church leadership so they can be revered as almost God Himself. Fear tactics are used to control the hurting people. Hurtful and abusive sermons are common to further manipulate. I had to remove myself from every norm I had. You see, partial freedom is not possible. You cannot be emotionally free, but not spiritually free. When God frees you, you become free in every area from every jail. It was the night Alaura was born when I told God I want to help heal this world for her and other children coming. With my baby in my arms, He told me that He would allow me to see what He sees. I did not understand then, but I understand today.

Once I began to see organized religion, I could no longer position myself there. I learned that religion is a metric system people use to measure how much others love God. The more religious events, activities, or traditions you maintain, the more religion says you love God. The fewer religious events you attend, the less you love God. Well, I found God outside of religion. He was waiting in the place I needed Him the most.

You see, I realized that God was never aiming to hurt me. He never aimed to destroy my marriage, my relationships with my family, or any of my relationships. He sought to tear down the religion I was born into, because that was my truest prison and I could never accomplish my purpose on this earth in it. I could not decipher the difference between my insecurities and the voice of God. I had spent my entire life in fear of disappointing God, but it was not God - it was religious dogma. Once I realized this, I retired from all church titles, positions, and roles.

I wanted to share that with others. My company grew even more successful as I purchased a new home. God placed me in a role sharing His hope, love, and peace with dozens of other business owners every day. I then began to rest my head on my pillow every night feeling my Father in Heaven was proud. Had I known God instead of religious practices, I would have never chased the women I chased in life. I did exactly what religion says one is supposed to do to live a blessed life, and when the formula did not work; I questioned myself. I never questioned God or religion because I was taught such an act warranted death. So, I questioned myself, and I aimed to fix myself. But when I learned that church practices could not heal me anymore than they healed all of the other people in my story, I knew I needed more. I am grateful that more existed. There are true men and women of the cloth who have sacrificed great wants and faced great fears to have a close intimate relationship with God. However, most of the times, they are not the popular figures exalted before the world as the image of godliness and faith.

Religion never required my father, mother, Nikki, Jeff, Gloria, Tonya, or myself to heal. Religion accepted and idolized all of our demons every Sunday. Religion does not hold one accountable, but God does. After I healed, I could no longer dwelled in any spaces where there were no boundaries.

Now, as my fully-grown self, you do not get to run amuck in my life. My life is not a wilderness, and I take my healing seriously. Therefore, there is no room for anyone with no regard for the boundaries that I have established to keep me on the path God chose for me. While I am not saying churches are not of God, I am saying that where the spirit of the Lord is, there is liberty. Where God is, there is liberty to establish boundaries. God is not sending you anywhere your *NO* cannot go. If you do not have the luxury of expressing what frightens, threatens, and harms you, then you do not have a circle of loved ones. You have a jail.

I had become addicted to the taste of healing in my soul. I found the sweetest healing comes through my ability to be vulnerable. My most vulnerable moments manifest themselves through my transparency. I had fallen in love with the simplicity of God and the pursuit of being my best self spiritually, physically, and emotionally.

It was only with this journey that I heard a truth only God could reveal. You see, after my divorce I learned how to identify toxic people. I was quick. I could spot a toxic jail-keeper a mile away, and if he or she got too close to my boundaries, I would stop them in their tracks. I proceeded forth in life feeling healed because God had given me the ability to recognize toxic people. So, I established strict, stern, and uncompromising boundaries with absolutely everyone. I drilled everyone who loved me to meet and respect those boundaries. The truth was, I had not healed. I had only learned how to identify the people and things that could hurt me, and instead of healing I projected unrealistic expectations on everyone around me to never do anything that made me feel afraid. Fear of being alone was still my prison, and whether it was a romantic partner, friend, or family member absolutely no one could meet my needs; not even God. I needed those who loved me to make me feel safe, and I needed that feeling often. I realized that I had lost many friendships and relationships because those who wanted to love me never stood a chance. While they wanted to love me, I only wanted them to make me feel safe. No amount of love would have been enough for me as long as I was still living in absolute fear. I knew Tonya did not love me. I could deal with that. I had never felt love so I would not miss it. But if she could make me feel safe, I would give her my all.

As I grew with God, I realized that I would always fail while loving from a place of fear. I had to come out of that jail. I had to reestablish my Basic Primary Needs. The needs I told myself were reasonable for anyone who loved me to meet, required others to sacrifice parts of themselves that they could never sacrifice. It was not their responsibility to make me feel safe. It was never Nikki, Adrianna, or Tonya's responsibility to make me feel safe no matter how much I insisted from them. I questioned people's faith, motives, character, and more if they could not make me feel safe. Then it all became clear. The safety, loyalty, and protection I still sought as a 35-year-old man was not in a spouse. It was my parents. It was never the responsibility of the women I loved, friends I made, or colleagues I met to make me feel safe. It was my parent's responsibility when I was just a child, and I spent the next 30 years looking for my parents in others. I then accepted that my parents did not and still could not give me what they did not have to give. I found safety in God.

I can now own the places where I was healed, and the places I still need to heal without shame. I was broken. Who would have thought that the success of my career, purpose, and ministry was ultimately linked to my darkest healing? The more vulnerable I became, the more I could speak truthfully of my life. The more I shared, the more I exited the jail of public opinion, and that is where my success rested. I had spent my entire life and career trying to balance the rules of religion with a purpose and gift planted in me by God. Whether through a production, mentoring, life coaching, or through business, I now serve people every day of various races, backgrounds, and beliefs. I serve them God. They may not know it, I may not say it, but because I serve them love, I serve them God.

My children are the most important beings to me. I became a father at a young age, and I pray that they can forgive me for not knowing what I did not know before I learned it.

I have now learned to give my children the freedom to set boundaries with me. I have learned that I will never be healed enough to allow my children to think I will not make a mistake. I remind them that they have the authority to stop me if I make them feel weak, hurt, or angry. I will not imprison their feelings to maintain my ego. They do not have to keep the secrets of my dysfunction. I remind them that there is no punishment or consequence for telling me' if I have disappointed or failed them. It is my belief that once we can establish healthy boundaries with our parents, then we will master doing the same with others. I want my children to be healthy in ways I could only dream of.

My parents now regularly tell me they are proud of my accomplishments. I do not know if they have the ability to see my most proud accomplishments. My accomplishments have nothing to do with my bank account, investments, company, brand, or belongings. My greatest accomplishment is being self-aware, and finally getting to see what God sees. After I had seen all the evil, hypocrisy, corruption, and filth imaginable in this world, He then filled my heart with love from all those performing the detestable acts. I felt not just forgiving love, but the type of love that would enable me to pray for their healing as well. Love removed my ability to hate. God's love enables me to view even the most damaged individuals as children who lost their way.

Still to this day, to some, all of my success is still accredited to the yellow of my skin. When I sell a production or develop a new company, a jail-keeper still finds his or her way to me to remind me that only a black man my complexion would be afforded such opportunities. Such ignorance no longer troubles me.

I will die loving Tonya. I have come to terms with that. It does not mean that I will never love another woman as a wife, but it is my belief that true love never dies- it transforms itself. Although I will never have romantic feelings for her, I love her as more than the mother of my children. I love her as a child of God, and I remind her that she is loved as such.

My entire healing would be in vain if I did not wish the most enriched healing upon her as well. I have no doubt that I made the best decision by ending the marriage. I freed her to pursue what makes her happy verses joining me in the jail I could not escape. There is enough love inside of me to spare. I am perfectly fine with always having love for her.

I have learned to love the yellow of my skin. I hated the color of my skin as a child, because I did not look like anyone else around me, and I believed my skin made me subject to abuse. My brothers gave me the nickname Yella Box when I was a child, and today it is the only remaining thing of my childhood that continues to make me smile. My brothers taught me to drive, ride a bicycle. They gave me all the protection they could give, but at times I resented them too for not protecting me. It was never their assignment, and I had to release them of my charge. I had to give them space to find their own paths to healing and growth as well. They still call me Yella Box today, and it reminds me of how far I have come. I hated the name as a child, but today it reminds me of my rebirth. I love it.

Most importantly, I no longer fight to find a stereotype of masculinity. I learned that toxic men think healthy men are not men at all. So, I gave myself permission to define masculinity to myself, and no one could rewrite my definition. My masculinity would be defined as my passionate love, care, and devotion to the people in my community. I defined masculinity as a man who does not run wild as a toxic man leaving a trail of broken men, women and children in his dust. I defined masculinity as a man so healed in his ability to love, that he has the ability to love those who cannot love themselves.

The art of my exit was truly God. God is real, and it took me a long time to finally find the God I knew existed somewhere beyond the world I had known. I was certain that God existed, but I had to find Him. I embarked on a twenty-nine-day fast where I consumed nothing but distilled water. I was determined to rid my body, mind, and spirit of everything toxic that I had allowed to enter me. With each passing day, my mind grew clearer. Around day twenty-four, I met God. He was not waiting, counting, or tracking the number of religious events I attended. He was not calculating monies I had placed in the collection plates. He was not counting the number of times I had fallen. I realized that even my dietary habits were contrary to the man God had created me to be. I adopted a plant-based diet, and for the first time in my life; my body and my soul both belonged to God. I lost almost one hundred pounds in nine months. I felt like God's masterpiece. You too are God's work of art. While I would love to promise you an easy healing after you follow the steps I shared, I cannot. You see, art is directly linked to pain. I can assure you that once you get a taste of what life is like healed and whole, you can never go back to only being a half.

The truest measure of your growth and healing reveals itself in your ability to tell your story in its most authentic truth without fear of judgement or ridicule. This is not a prison that you can exit quietly out the back door. I can now own and acknowledge all of my toxic behaviors, because I see they can no longer serve me post healing. I had to expose myself so that those who truly loved me could aid in holding me accountable in never returning to the man I once was. I decided many years ago that I would boldly stand toe-to-toe with every generational curse and toxic ideology that plagued my family with suffering for the last one hundred years. My parents did all they knew to do in all the ways they knew to do them. I believe their parents did the same. We were never told or taught that abuse was wrong. We were never told to never tolerate abuse or abuse others. So, as loudly as I can tell my story, I will do so. For my children, I will scream my story from the mountaintop to the bottom of the valley.

Release yourself. Whether you are twenty years old or eighty years old, release yourself. Tell your story. Once you release the shame, you can begin your new life.

You will weep, and you will ache. You will feel as if the world around you has forsaken you, but you will heal. You will heal in ways that you never knew healing could exist. You deserve to experience God's purpose for your life at your physical, spiritual, and emotional best. You can find God.

I found Him painted in vibrant colors of love, joy, peace, and finally, security. He was waiting beneath all the hurt, the pain, and the shame. He was there.


THE END